S0-CFZ-319

SHIRLEY TEMPLE

SHIRLEY TEMPLE

A Pyramid Illustrated History of the Movies

by
JEANINE BASINGER

General Editor: **TED SENNETT**

PYRAMID
PUBLICATIONS
NEW YORK

SHIRLEY TEMPLE
A Pyramid Illustrated History of the Movies

Copyright © 1975 by Pyramid Communications, Inc.

All rights reserved. No part of this book may be reproduced in any form or by any electronic or mechanical means including information storage and retrieval systems without permission in writing from the Publisher, except by a reviewer who may quote brief passages in a review.

Pyramid edition published February 1975

ISBN 0-515-03643-9

Library of Congress Catalog Card Number:

Printed in the United States of America

Pyramid Books are published by Pyramid Communications, Inc. Its trademarks, consisting of the word "Pyramid" and the portrayal of a pyramid, are registered in the United States Patent Office.

Pyramid Communications, Inc., 919 Third Avenue, New York, N.Y. 10022

CONDITIONS OF SALE

"Any sale, lease, transfer or circulation of this book by way of trade or in quantities of more than one copy, without the original cover bound thereon, will be construed by the Publisher as evidence that the parties to such transaction have illegal possession of the book, and will subject them to claim by the Publisher and prosecution under the law."

(graphic design by anthony basile)

ACKNOWLEDGMENTS

I am blessed with the best and most generous of friends. I wish to thank all of them for their help with films, stills, advice, suggestions, and moral support. William K. Everson, Leonard Maltin, Gary Collins, Steve Ross, Patricia Moore, Chris Baffer. Also Joseph Duseault, Loraine Burdick, (whom I don't know, but whose books on Shirley Temple were very helpful) and Stanley Stark of United Artists Television. Thanks for help with research, typing, and copying to Mrs. Peter Arico, Bette Zuraw, Ted Hoey, Milton Rome, and Edith Shaffrick.

Special thanks to Gerald Haber of Hartford, who was simply invaluable. Also to Douglas Lemza of Films, Incorporated, who has helped me not only with this book, but with many past efforts. His knowledge and support of film history are truly commendable.

No book or film project of any sort could be complete for me without giving thanks to my dear, dear friends at the University of Connecticut Film Society: Robert E. Smith, Jeffrey Wise, and Michael Geragotelis. Thanks to them for their devotion to films and for the many kind deeds and marvelous conversations over the years.

Last of all, thanks to my good husband, John, who helped in every possible way and whose suggestions made all the difference, and to our daughter, Savannah, who was patient.

Photographs: Jerry Vermilye, The Memory Shop,
Movie Star News, Kier Photos, Gerald Haber, Gene Andrewski,
The Museum of Modern Art—Still Collection,
and Columbia Pictures

CONTENTS

I class myself with Rin Tin Tin. People were looking for something to cheer them up. They fell in love with a dog and a little girl.

Shirley Temple Black

INTRODUCTION: LITTLE MISS MONEYBAGS

Some are stars, and others are superstars. Some are sadly relegated forever to that ignominious category of "starlet." A few reach mythic proportions or are considered "living legends." There are overnight successes and has-beens, forgotten faces and subjects for where-are-they-now columns. Gods and goddesses or flashes in the pan—all are part of the colorful history of Hollywood. But virtually alone and certainly unique is that cultural phenomenon of the 1930's, Miss Shirley Temple, also known as Little Miss Miracle, Curly Top, and Golden Hawk, Little Spirit of the Sun.

In her day, Shirley Temple had a box-office stature twice that of Greta Garbo. She was known all over the world, and her name as endorsement guaranteed sales of everything from baby soap to Bisquick. She was more than a movie star—she was an American folk heroine who sat in the lap of the President and ate hamburgers at Hyde Park. Even people who never went to the movies knew her and loved her. Today her films are revived consistently and successfully. She is the only Hollywood star who

rates regular television revivals on every station in the country, as The Shirley Temple Theatre plays to each new generation. Yet nobody takes her seriously . . .

Like others who represent the special madness of their times —Esther Williams, Nelson Eddy and Jeanette MacDonald, or Carmen Miranda—Shirley Temple is considered unworthy of thought by people who have grown up and now know better. She has been variously written off as "a schmaltzy sweetmeat" . . . "a golden-haired pterodactyl" . . . or "a sentimental legend . . . driven home with a stake through the heart."

In truth, there's very little to recommend most of her movies. They usually have no stunning technique to make them interesting from a formalist viewpoint, or to endear them to "camp" enthusiasts. They were rarely directed by men acceptable to auteurist critics. Some were undistinguished in terms of sets, costumes, co-stars, or scripts. Often they were little more than a sentimental bath in a kiddie pool.

The Shirley Temple film followed a standard format. Shirley played an orphaned child adopted by a rich

father . . . or rich mother . . . or perhaps a rich grandfather or grandmother. Or she played a child whose mother was dead and whose father wandered off absentmindedly, leaving her to cope. She was torn out of the arms of benefactor after benefactor ("Oh, please, Cap, don't let them take me away" . . . "I want my daddy" . . . "No, no, I don't want to go to any old orphanage"). This basic ingredient of the child alone was mixed together with crusts of old codgers, heaps of adoring adults, pinches of heartbreak, and generous helpings of cheerful poverty (which quickly melted into lavish living)—all stirred up with the subtlety of a McCormick reaper and garnished with a few songs and dances. That was the recipe for a Shirley Temple movie, and it was good enough to satisfy movie-going appetites for nearly six years of top stardom.

Were we a nation of idiots? Why did people trek like lemmings into movie houses to indulge themselves in the sight of this little girl's tiny toes tapping, her innocent curls bouncing, and her chipmunk cheeks dimpling? How could she forge a major career out of nothing but a child's uncanny ability to disarm adults?

There was one simple reason: as a very small child, Shirley Temple was terrific. It wasn't the movies she made that mattered—it was her.

She was a little girl who glowed in the dark, and as Darryl Zanuck correctly pointed out: "Her films didn't make her—she made them." No matter how clichéd the plot . . . talented or untalented her co-stars . . . gorgeous or ordinary the sets and costumes . . . it didn't really matter, as long as she herself was up there on the screen.

Shirley Temple was literally a living doll. From the tips of her fifty-five golden corkscrew curls (as natural as could be) to the tips of her patent-leather toes, she was all dimples, bright eyes, and sunny smile. Her little body was roundly formed, with a pair of smooth thighs always visible beneath the short, short dresses which barely grazed the bottoms of her ruffled underpants. And if the most famous under-pinups of the forties belonged to Betty Grable—in the thirties the Hollywood legs to look at belonged to Dietrich . . . and little Shirley Temple. She had an adult's control over her body and a definition to her gestures that were beyond her age. For nearly six years she managed to make time stand still, as she miraculously maintained a balance between adorable child and vamping coquette.

On screen, Shirley Temple wasn't just another child, she was the all-American child. She embodied those old-fashioned virtues of candor and common sense that

Americans prize. Although her films were sometimes sticky sweet, she seldom was. She was a salty little wench, full of fun and mischief, who seized hold of situations and straightened them out for herself. Never cowed by authority, she dealt with presidents and queens as she did bootblacks and butlers, dishing out finger-waggling lectures and telling them off right and left. The number of judges, sheriffs, bankers, business tycoons, and doctors she straightened out was more than legion—it was downright embarrassing. She was the greatest little democrat of them all.

Shirley Temple was the American pioneer spirit personified, as she forged a path of cheerful dominance through the grimmest of situations. When a crisis came, she was ready for it—bravely marching through graveyards at midnight or racing on foot to bring help. Nannies were run over, leaving her stranded. Ships sank under her tap-dancing feet. Fathers put bullets in their brains. The orphan asylum was either just around the corner or already a painful reality, but Shirley rolled on with a cheery "Oh, my goodness" and a crunch on one of her animal crackers. "I'm very self-reliant, you know," she said in *Rebecca of Sunnybrook Farm*, and so she was. Not much frightened her and practically nothing stopped her. And although

she couldn't really qualify as a liberated female, she shed remarkably few tears and never once swooned in a pinch.

Besides that sunny good cheer, though, what else brought so many people into the theatres? Beneath the surface of her screen image lurked hidden, disturbing messages. That she was an out-and-out baby sexpot was pointed out even in her own day, as her constantly kissing little mouth unquestionably held an adult's promise. Today it is almost impossible to overlook the oddity of her playing "little wife" and keeping house for her own father. Or, worse yet, sitting in his lap and singing "Marry me and let me be your wife." And how many incestuous nightmares were fed by her warbling to Papa, "In every dream I caress you."

But although her sex appeal is undeniable, it wasn't really that which drew adults to her. In one of her most successful films, *Captain January*, her old benefactor, Guy Kibbee, has a dream fantasy. He sees himself as a baby in a high chair, while Shirley Temple feeds him from a bowl. And there it was, right out in the open: her films fed the public their Pablum. The adult's fantasy was not so much to have a little girl like her (although that might do), but to actually *be* her. To be taken care of, fussed over, listened to. And, above all in those

dark days of the Depression when she was the princess royal, to have financial woes solved by some rich old father figure. Nowhere is the wish fulfillment Hollywood sold more painfully revealed than in these movies which used a little child as the dream merchant. The wish to be rich, to be loved, to be respected and honored, but also to be a child—the total escape.

Even further inside the candied apple was the rotten core. In a film where children could participate as equals to adults, there was the hint of the American dream gone sour. Within every rich tycoon was the soul of a little boy who wanted to be young again. There was the dissatisfied adult who had pursued the goal of success but had nothing that mattered to show for it. As adults watched, they felt better about having been neglected as children; they relived a better childhood through her. And their own children, the new neglected generation, found escape from their own lonely lives, as they, too, identified.

In the golden era of Hollywood, girls had a chance at stardom if they were exceptionally good-looking. If they were lucky, they could take hold, forge a distinct style of their own—and endure. Shirley Temple reversed that formula. As a child, she burst upon the public already a star personality. As an adult, she was just another pretty face.

So sexy as a small child—so full of life—she grew up to be curiously bland. And although she looked almost exactly the same, nobody wanted to look at her anymore. No one cared how she grew. With Elizabeth Taylor, it was the hint of the woman-to-be within her extraordinary youth that drew attention. People couldn't wait to see her as a grown-up, and they loved her even better when she fulfilled her childish promise of rare beauty. With Judy Garland, it was the strain of vulnerability. Would she grow up or not? Could she make it? The drama of her struggle to mature was almost as entertaining as her enormous talent. But with Shirley Temple, there was no place to grow but up . . . and out.

We locked the little princess in the tower and threw away the key. If we couldn't retain our innocence, at least we'd keep the proof that once we'd had it. Shirley Temple became America's official little girl, forever young on Saturday afternoons and late, late at night, to remind us that, although there may never have been a Camelot, at least there was a Peppermint Bay. Needless to say, we will never see her like again.

Shirley's film career was thrust upon her. We never thought of it.

Gertrude Temple,
Screenland Magazine, 1934

"WHEN I WAS THREE AND UNKNOWN..."

Shirley Jane Temple was born —so she and the rest of the world believed—on April 23, 1929. On her twelfth birthday she was told she had actually been born on April 23, 1928, and as was traditional for female box-office champions, a year had been sliced off her age. As was also traditional, the movie-going world was let in on the secret somewhat later, but by that time they didn't care anyway. Shirley Jane Temple had become "our girl Shirley," and if her incredible talent had initially been the precociousness of a four-year-old instead of a three-year-old—what difference did it make? She was still remarkable!

The beginning of her life, however, was not remarkable. Unlike such famous show-business youngsters as Judy Garland and Mickey Rooney, she was not "born in a trunk." Nor was she born into the sophisticated world of international art dealers, like Elizabeth Taylor. Nor was she the daughter of a frustrated actress, as was Jane Withers, whose mother accepted a proposal of marriage only on the condition that, if a baby girl were born, she would be trained for a theatrical career. On the contrary, Shirley

Temple was born into a quiet-living family of modest means whose members had no experience whatsoever in the world of entertainment.

Shirley's father, George Temple, was from Pennsylvania Dutch stock, and his straight-living and sober-sided manner matched all that such a background might indicate. His wife Gertrude, whom he met while she was a student at a Los Angeles High School, was the daughter of a former Chicago jeweler. The Temples were married when Gertrude was only seventeen (as Shirley herself would be later), and despite economic hardships in their early married years, had done moderately well. Mr. Temple had become a teller at a Santa Monica Bank. The couple had two children, Jack and George, who were ages fourteen and ten, respectivly, when Shirley was born. At that time the family was living in a small one-story white stucco house, and although they owned their own car, the house had a mortgage on it. When Shirley Jane was born, the child of the Temples' later married life, she was adored and doted upon—the only girl in a family which already boasted two fine sons.

Shirley at age three

Shirley was a sunny and pretty child, who, according to Mrs. Temple's descriptions, glided along on her toes rather than just walking or running like other children. "Long before she was born," Mrs. Temple later told an interviewer, "I tried to influence her future life by association with music, art, and natural beauty. Perhaps this prenatal preparation helped make Shirley what she is today." As Norman Zierold remarked in his book on child stars, "It is one of the few documented cases we have of a stage mother operating at the prenatal stage."

The proximity of their home to the golden hills of Hollywood naturally had its effect on the Temples' life. Whether it was Mrs. Temple who insisted that Shirley be given dancing lessons, or it was suggested to Mr. Temple by a bank customer—or if it were just fate —the stories differ, and no one is really sure. What is known is that, by the age of three, Shirley Temple was enrolled as a regular customer in one of Los Angeles' hundreds of tap-dancing factories for potential Jackie Coogans. Despite the pinched times for the family purse, little Shirley was going to be given her opportunity to make the small-set big time. (Later, Mrs. Temple was to insist that the dancing lessons were only for Shirley to "keep up with her brothers.")

At that point in the history of Hollywood, with the studios booming and the industry hardly feeling the bite of the Depression's big bad wolf, talent scouts were everywhere. It was inevitable that one would show up at Shirley's dancing school. As she herself tells it, "I remember when I was three and unknown and some character who turned out to be a talent scout came into dancing school and I hid under the piano. Obviously no poise. He stood around for a while watching and then he said, 'I'll take the one under the piano.' " "He" was Charles Lamont, a director and talent scout for Educational Films, and when he spotted Shirley Temple under a piano, he proved himself to be a talent scout with x-ray vision. Lamont was looking for a group of talented children, none taller than thirty-six inches, to star in a series of shorts to be called "The Baby Burlesks."

Mrs. Temple recalls, "Three days later a little film company down in the older quarter of Hollywood, in what is known to the big league as Poverty Row, telephoned me and asked me to bring Shirley in for a screen test. When I told George about it, he hit the ceiling, but later he good-naturedly gave his consent to letting Shirley make the test. Three days after that test, she was selected to play a part in a one-reel juvenile comedy, *War Babies,* which was to launch an educational series of such films. Her salary was to be ten dollars per day, four days a week. When I told George that, he hit the ceiling again—with joy!"

With this contract, Shirley Temple began her years as a "working tot," and Mrs. Temple was ready for the challenge. She had already learned to drive a car in order to chauffeur Shirley back and forth to her dance class. Having faced the California traffic, she was ready for any kind of burlesque her baby was required to do, especially at forty dollars per week.

The Baby Burlesks were a product of Educational Films, an "on-the-cheap" shorts studio that ground out one- and two-reelers of varying quality. Educational had been founded in 1919 with the idea of making films for distribution in American elementary and secondary schools (hence the studio name). The idea had not worked out, and Educational had become a short-comedy factory. The studio ads told the whole story: "The best of the old comedy favorites and the brightest of the new stars." In other words, Educational gave them a boost up the ladder and was there to catch them when they fell back down.

Lamont wasted no time in putting Shirley to work. The Baby Burlesks series was designed to feature small children in satires on the adult

KID'S
LAST FIGHT
(1933)

WAR BABIES (1932)

WB-9
21001-23

GLAD RAGS TO RICHES (1932)

box-office hits of the day. Unlike the successful Our Gang comedies (whose enormous popularity may have inspired the idea, however), Baby Burlesks were not necessarily *for* children. The idea was to use the kiddies to amuse adults, and seen today, the series seems distinctly exploitative. The children wore adult costumes on the top halves of their bodies: hats, gloves, furs, jewelry. Underneath they were decked out in diapers which were pinned in the front with gigantic safety pins. Chubby little legs clad

in high-heeled shoes or heavy boots stuck out beneath, creating a ludicrous comic effect. Shirley made four Baby Burlesks in 1932: *War Babies*, a satire on *What Price Glory?*; *The Runt Page*, a spoof of *The Front Page* which was allegedly never released theatrically; *Pie Covered Wagon*, which ran ten minutes and worked off *The Covered Wagon*; and *Glad Rags to Riches*, a Gay Nineties episode.

In *War Babies*, Shirley Temple uttered her first screen words, "Mais oui, mon cher!"—and later admitted she didn't know what it was supposed to mean. (There were other problems of understanding for a tiny tot. "I remember that first day on the set as clear as anything. I heard the director tell somebody to get the dolly ready and I waited for a blue-eyed baby doll to show up. When it turned out to be a little cart to carry the camera, I cried my heart out. . . . Once I heard someone say, 'Put the baby in the fireplace' and I was so scared I started to run until they explained it meant a little spotlight.")

Glad Rags to Riches is a typical Baby Burlesk. Shirley plays La Belle Diaperina, lovely chanteuse of the Lullabye Lobster Palace. Billed as "the spice of the program," that is exactly what she is—the pepper as well as the sugar. Blonder than she often looks, Shirley wears a Gay Nineties hat and a typical

On the Paramount lot, 1934

turn-of-the-century "show girl" costume. After singing "Only a Bird in a Gilded Cage," she executes a tap dance with extraordinary skill. The nonsensical storyline involved La Belle Diaperina, formerly farm girl Little Nell, rescued from "a fate worse than death" by her hayseed lover.

As 1932 rolled along, Shirley proved herself a valuable source of income to the Temple family during the depth of the Depression. The Baby Burlesks were a success, and Shirley's parents signed a contract with Jack Hays (the series producer and supervisor)—a contract which was the basis of a lawsuit after she became a top star (with the Temples winning).

During the run of her work with Educational during 1932, Shirley was loaned out to Tower Productions to play a small part in *Red-Haired Alibi,* which starred Merna Kennedy, Grant Withers, and Theodor Von Eltz. Released by the Capital Films Exchange, it is the one about the girl set up in luxury by a gangster, who later sees the light and marries her small-town sweetheart. Shirley's footage was small, but she now had a feature film on her list of credits. By the end of 1932, Gertrude Temple was firmly convinced that Shirley would be a star, and mother and daughter were off on the traditional round of visits to casting offices, armed with photos, previous credits, and tap shoes.

The odds against any child becoming a star in those days were estimated at 15,000 to 1, but the Temples had a lot going for them. In addition to the bright eyes, curly top, and dimples of the little princess Mrs. Temple had in tow, there was the fact that Shirley was already established in the business. Even more important, they lived in the Hollywood area already and didn't have to risk everything on the trip West as so many hopeful families did. (Hedda Hopper described the beribboned tots in tutus who were brought to California as "a flock of hungry locusts, driven by the gale winds of their pushing, prompting, ruthless mothers." Hopper added, "I used to wonder if there wasn't a special subhuman species of womankind that bred children for the sole purpose of dragging them to Hollywood."

Nothing discouraged these mothers, and nothing discouraged Mrs. Temple either. Although cut from quite a different cloth than the harpies the gossip columnist had described, she was, in her own quiet way, a determined and resolute woman. By virtue of a dancing class, the Temples had been summoned. And like one of those intricate military tap numbers for which Shirley was later so famous, the event was underway—to rap, tap along to its finale with no interference from anyone and without the baby's missing a single step or ever once forgetting to flash her dimpled smile.

My God! Another Coogan!
Harold Lloyd, 1934

GOOD MORNING, STAR CHILD!

The year 1933 opened with the Depression at its lowest point, Mr. Temple's bank on the brink of closing, and Shirley gainfully, if not tastefully, employed at Educational. During the year, she was to tuck four more Baby Burlesks under her diapers: _Kid's Last Fight, Kid'in' Hollywood, Polly-Tix in Washington,_ and _Kid'in' Africa._ Of these, _Kid'in' Hollywood_ was probably the best (and the least offensive), a backstage Hollywood story with Shirley as a former beauty-contest winner, reduced to scrubbing the sound-stage floors, who is turned into the incomparable Morelegs Sweetrick by director Frightwig Von Stumblebum. In _Polly-Tix in Washington,_ the four-year-old Shirley plays what can only be described as a call girl, decked out in black-lace bra and panties and mouthing dialogue apparently written by Mae West.

After these Burlesks, Shirley appeared in an Andy Clyde two-reeler called _Dora's Dunkin' Doughnuts._ Clyde, a Scotsman who had worked for Mack Sennett, played a lovable hick character in a series of successful Educational shorts. In this one, he is a schoolteacher who tries to promote his sweetheart's homemade doughnuts (They Float!). Shirley steals the show as one of his younger students who breaks up his radio debut with her rendition of a Durante-like "Ha-cha-cha!" at key moments. _Dora's Dunkin' Doughnuts_ is most notable as the first screen glimpse of the real Shirley, the little moppet whose natural smile and good timing made her a box-office champion.

To finish out 1933, Shirley appeared as Little Sister in one of Educational's "Frolics of Youth" two-reelers (_Merrily Yours_), and was loaned out twice for small parts in feature films. At Paramount, she appeared as Barton MacLane and Gail Patrick's daughter in Henry Hathaway's _To the Last Man,_ and she was a child checked in a department-store nursery supervised by ZaSu Pitts in Universal's comedy, _Out All Night._

Early in 1934, Shirley was given a part in a Paramount short (a two-reeler) called _New Deal Rhythm_ with Charles "Buddy" Rogers and Marjorie Main. It was an inexpensive way for Paramount to "screen test" Shirley and sample public reaction to her at the same time. Having just purchased Damon Runyon's popular story, "Little Miss Marker," (Alexander

KID 'IN' HOLLYWOOD (1933)

Hall was set to direct), Paramount was looking for the right little girl for the title role. Studio powers had suggested the part be made over for a boy (they hoped to borrow Jackie Cooper from Metro), but Hall was against this idea.

In the meantime, Shirley finished her work at Educational, making two more "Frolics of Youth" two-reelers as Little Sister. The first was *Pardon My Pups*, and the second, in which she co-starred with Junior Coghlan, was *Managed Money*. Her memories of her days as a burlesque queen are vivid. "In one I was dumped in a cart behind an ostrich whose blindfold was then yanked off. I was scared to death. In another I was a 'lady explorer'

being chased by Negro extras who were supposed to be cannibals. They were tripped by an invisible wire and landed in a great scattered heap—everybody in tears. No wonder they didn't allow mothers on the set!"

Two small parts in features were next. At Fox, she was unbilled in a tiny role as a sharecropper's child in Henry King's *Carolina*, a film version of Paul Green's play, *The House of Connelly*, starring Janet Gaynor, Lionel Barrymore, and Robert Young. She was equally unnoticeable in a bit part over at Warner Brothers in Michael Curtiz' *Mandalay*, with Kay Francis and Ricardo Cortez. She was, however, working steadily, and

POLLY-TIX IN WASHINGTON (1933)

PARDON MY PUPS (1934). With George Chandler

Mother Temple always had her eye out for the big one which could make the difference in her little girl's career.

One night Leo Houck, assistant director at the Fox studios where Shirley had come for tryouts, met Shirley and her mother in a movie-theatre lobby. They had come to see her latest short in release (*Managed Money*). After the show, Houck introduced Shirley and her mother to Jay Gorney, a songwriter who was looking for a little girl to play James Dunn's daughter in a Fox picture to be called *Fox Movietone Follies*. Since her short films had already established her singing and dancing ability, Shirley seemed a natural choice. At Fox, Lew Brown (Gorney's partner) auditioned her and selected her for the role.

Gorney and Brown rehearsed Shirley carefully in her number, costumed her, and brought her onto

the set to "try out" for Winfield Sheehan, Fox's vice president in charge of production. Shirley's mother later recalled this important audition: "It was perfectly done. Even I was thrilled. Harold Lloyd was standing in the back with me. He was saying 'My God! Another Coogan.' Then someone asked, 'Has she got an agent?'" Sheehan was deeply impressed, and signed her to a one-picture contract at $150 per week, and *Stand Up and Cheer* (as *Fox Movietone Follies* was retitled) went into production.

After Shirley Temple became a big star, a somewhat different "discovery" story was given out by the studio. In this more legendary version, little Shirley and her mother are innocent visitors to the set of *Follies*. Spotted by Gorney, Shirley is asked if she can sing and dance, and while busy executives ignore her, she quickly memorizes the words to "Baby, Take a Bow," which are handed to her on the back of an envelope. When someone questioned this . . . after all, how could little Shirley *read* those words . . . the story had an addendum: Mrs. Temple read the words on the envelope slowly to her, so she could learn them!

Whatever really did happen that day, Shirley Temple was indeed assigned the plum role in the revue-like *Stand Up and Cheer,* a film which now makes a perfect showcase to learn why Shirley Temple became a star. In the middle of a very ramshackle movie, she dances in, as fresh as clover, dainty and dimpled and looking like everyone's little dream child—a girl who keeps her dress clean and never forgets to smile.

Stand Up and Cheer was based on an idea by Will Rogers and Philip Klein. The plot concerns the appointment of a Secretary of Amusement (Warner Baxter) to restore laughter and self-confidence to the American people during the dark days of the Depression. It is full of old-fashioned vaudeville routines, unfunny comedy attempts, and downright distasteful episodes (such as Stepin Fetchit's jumping into a large fish tank "looking for a halibut"). Shirley's number, however, seems modern. Unlike some of the other musical interludes, it does not rely on fancy optical effects to carry it. Furthermore, it is attractively designed in a black-and-white moderne motif, with silvery touches of chrome and sparkling sequins against black velvet. The first portion of the number ("Baby, Take a Bow") features an army of chorus girls and James Dunn (who sings along enthusiastically, unaware he is just about to become the picture's official "forgotten man"). When Shirley taps out on stage, wearing a highly starched polka-dot dress, she is like a little

STAND UP AND CHEER (1934). As Shirley Dugan

doll come to life. Precocious without being overly cute, she delivers her variation of the song ("Daddy, Take a Bow") with great timing and no sense of fighting to remember lyrics. She dances with speed and grace, and while some of her later routines (which were more complicated) seem to be carefully tapped out to prevent mistakes, this number shows her to be a little girl who not only could dance but who genuinely enjoyed dancing.

With its rousing call to Americans to "stand up and cheer" in the face of economic disaster, and its incredible finale of relentlessly marching American workers of all types and occupations, *Stand Up and Cheer* is as close as Hollywood ever came to Leni Riefenstahl's Nazi propaganda film *Triumph of the Will,* but in a contrived film that is a pure period piece, Shirley Temple alone seems easy and polished. The baby could indeed take a bow—little Shirley Temple had stolen the show!

After the completion of *Stand Up and Cheer,* Gertrude Temple knew that her golden-curled daughter was a "hot property." Following an impulse, she took Shirley to visit Alexander Hall, and her hunch was rewarded with the overwhelming good news that Shirley could have the lead role in *Little Miss Marker.*

Mrs. Temple was overjoyed. She naturally assumed that if the movie were a hit, Paramount would put Shirley under a long-term contract. But over at Fox, Winfield Sheehan had already seen the rushes of *Stand Up and Cheer,* and he shrewdly signed Shirley to a seven-year contract before Paramount had a chance. Those seven years—in which Shirley grew from age six to age thirteen—turned out to be the seven golden years of her reign as a child star.

While Fox writers E. E. Paramore, Jr., and Philip Klein designed a starring film for her, Shirley did two more bit parts at the studio, her last as anything but a leading lady. In *Change of Heart,* based on Kathleen Norris' "Manhattan Love Song," she had a small role with stars Janet Gaynor, Charles Farrell, and Ginger Rogers. She also appeared in *Now I'll Tell,* a melodrama with Spencer Tracy and Helen Twelvetrees, based on Mrs. Arnold Rothstein's true story about her husband. But since no script was ready for her, Fox decided to lend her out to the patient Paramount for Hall's *Little Miss Marker*—a move that paid off in more than dollars, for it was the film that made her a star. Paramount returned the little bundle to Fox wrapped up, as it were, in cloth of gold.

About her first starring role, Shirley has said, "*Little Miss Marker* was a real tear-jerker. Adolphe Menjou was wonderful to work

LITTLE MISS MARKER (1934). With Warren Hymer and Adolphe Menjou

with. He used to play jacks and hide-and-seek with me, but the games ended the day he sailed over a portable fence and landed on his face."

Menjou, the first of the hard-bitten older men who were thawed out on film by the Temple charms, told an interviewer during production: "I've played with a lot of actresses, and I've learned how to defend myself. You know, troupers who step on your lines and steal your scenes. But this child frightens me. She knows all the tricks. She backs me out of the camera, blankets me, crabs my laughs—she's making a stooge of me. Why, if she were forty years old and on the stage all her life, she wouldn't have had the time to learn all she knows about acting. Don't ask me how she does it. You've heard of chess champions at eight and violin virtuosos at ten? Well, she's an Ethel Barrymore at six."*

Menjou was right. An immortal moment takes place on screen in

*Gene Ringgold, *Screen Facts*, Vol. 2, No. 6, 1965.

Little Miss Marker. While Dorothy Dell is singing her big number atop a piano, a little girl walks up beside her and draws the audience's full attention. "Scram, kid, you're crabbin' my act," hisses Dorothy. It might well have become the motto of adult actors in Hollywood from that day on, as "little Ethel" stole the spotlight and put it in her pinafore pocket for good and all.

Little Miss Marker is one of Shirley Temple's more delightful pictures, despite a sentimental ending with a maudlin prayer scene by Menjou (surely one of the actors least likely to pray in any given situation). It has Damon Runyon's familiar characteristics: a collection of lovable hoodlums with unlikely names like Sore Toe, Regret, Bangles, Sorrowful, and Benny the Gouge, all delivering dialogue that is as spicy as it is funny. These underworld characters and their salty wit offset the Victorian quality of the story about a little girl who is left as an I.O.U. marker by a father who

LITTLE MISS MARKER (1934). With Dorothy Dell and Adolphe Menjou

later commits suicide. (The child's mother is already dead, obviously of that strange malady that strikes the on-screen mothers of child stars —on-screen mothers being as apparently vulnerable as their off-screen counterparts were indestructible.)

The true talent of the picture—and its most charming ingredient—is Shirley Temple. She plays with genuine freshness and remarkable timing. Her offhanded delivery of underworld jargon ("Aw, lay off me," she tells Dorothy Dell, who is trying to feed her mush) is totally non-precious. She is as cute as any child on screen has ever been or could ever expect to be. In addition, she sings a pleasant song ("Laugh, You Son-of-a-Gun") and remains calm in the face of a bucking horse and a blood transfusion. Unfortunately, the ending is treacly and not up to the smart-talking pace set in the earlier portion of the film by the excellent supporting cast. Besides Menjou, there was the young Dorothy Dell (a cross between Mae West and Thelma Todd, who died tragically in an automobile accident soon after this film marked her for stardom) plus Charles Bickford and Lynne Overman.

Little Miss Marker was a smash hit, garnering reviews for Shirley that made Sheehan's mouth water. Referred to in the plot as "forty and a half pounds of trouble," Miss Shirley Temple was from that day forward nothing but forty-plus pounds of good luck for her home studio.

When the spirit of the people is lower than any other time during this Depression, it is a splendid thing that for just fifteen cents an American can go to a movie and look at the smiling face of a baby and forget his troubles.

President Franklin
Delano Roosevelt

ON THE GOOD SHIP SHIRLEY TEMPLE

Shirley Temple was no longer just Shirley Jane Temple, adored youngest child of the George Temple family of Santa Monica. She was now SHIRLEY TEMPLE, MOVIE STAR, and her home studio (Fox Films) rushed her into her next picture. Titled *Baby, Take a Bow* (to capitalize on her hit number from *Stand Up and Cheer*), it was a sentimental story about an ex-convict trying to make a good life for himself and his family (Claire Trevor and Temple). Not content with just using the title to remind the audience of Shirley's success in *Stand Up and Cheer*, Fox also paired her again with James Dunn. The two of them performed an audience-pleasing duet, this time called "On Accounta I Love You."

Following this film, which did well at the box office, Fox again lent Shirley to Paramount for a movie which was called *Honor Bright* during production, but was released as *Now and Forever*. Anxious to keep their new little star working (and well aware of what Paramount

had done for her with *Little Miss Marker*), Fox was only too happy to have her co-starred off the home-lot with such luminaries as Gary Cooper and Carole Lombard. Shirley is billed third, after the two adults, but still over the title. *Now and Forever*, however, is the sort of film which could have killed her career before it really got started.

Paramount seemed to have ambivalent feelings about making another film to boost the little Fox star, and obviously did not want to neglect its own two contract players at her expense. *Now and Forever* is almost two different stories: one comic and melodramatic, the other stickily sentimental. In the beginning, it is a fast-paced business about two sophisticated international wanderers, a slick con man and his devoted companion. (There is some ambiguity about the Cooper/Lombard relationship. It is never stated that they are married, although they are obviously living together. The cast list gives Lombard the same last name as Cooper, a last-minute touch rumored to be a sop to critics who complained about Shirley's being seen in such seedy company.) After a promising open-

BABY, TAKE A BOW (1934). With Claire Trevor

ing section involving a neat and im-aginative swindle of a Shanghai hotel, brought off beautifully by Cooper, the film plunges rapidly into bathos and boredom.

Suddenly the con man turns out to have a little daughter back in Connecticut (whose mother has just conveniently died), and she joins the couple on their travels, creating a weird *ménage à trois*. The film ends with Shirley off to school with her new benefactress (a rich old lady of the sort who were always waiting in the wings to give her everything she needed) and Cooper off to jail for theft and murder. The implica-tion is that Lombard will stick by him and they will all eventually live happily ever after. The split between the adult story and the more sentimental, even mawkish story of the little girl, is nowhere more apparent than in Shirley's one big musical number ("The World Owes Me a Living"). In the middle of her routine, the camera cuts away to show Cooper's stealing a necklace and hiding it in her teddy bear.

Now and Forever is a dull, slackly paced film. Cooper and Lombard, two of the most charming players of the 1930's, seem bored with the assignment. The only real charm of the picture is derived from the playing of six-year-old Shirley Temple, who, because of her diminutive size, looks even younger. But no matter how much sunny smiling or coy finger-waggling Shirley does, showing herself to be a natural-born trouper with an uncanny sense of timing, nothing can save the overall film.

Back at Fox, Shirley went immediately into her next movie, which, unlike *Now and Forever*, required no "star names" as protection and was the first movie built totally around her. (Although *Baby, Take a Bow* used her hit song as its title, she was not really the center of the action.) *Bright Eyes* was for Shirley and about Shirley—even her character's name was Shirley. From the first moment she appears,

NOW AND FOREVER (1934). With Gary Cooper

hitchhiking down a country road in a miniature pilot's cap, the baby has the situation well in hand. *Bright Eyes* was the first "typical Shirley Temple film"—a relatively trite story brought to the screen with an undistinguished screenplay, undistinguished design and photography, and equally undistinguished performances. The notable exception is Temple herself, who, considering her age and what was required of her, can't really be considered anything but remarkable.

Many think of *Bright Eyes* as one of Shirley's best films. Among its assets are a wittily drawn crank character, instead of a sentimental portrait of a rough old man with a marshmallow interior. This character, played by Charles Sellon, is a true W. C. Fields type* who bumps himself downstairs in his wheelchair, calls himself plain Mr. Smith (his *nouveau riche* relatives have changed it to Smythe), and insists on reminding everyone his money was made "in sewers." Shirley sings one of her all-time biggest hits—the one song that is probably most often

*In fact, in Fields' 1934 comedy, *It's A Gift*, Sellon played the blind Mr. Muckle who demolishes Fields' store with his cane.

NOW AND FOREVER (1934). With Gary Cooper, Carole Lombard, and Charlotte Granville

BRIGHT EYES (1934). With Jane Withers

associated with her: "On the Good Ship Lollipop." The song is delivered aboard a taxiing airplane, where her birthday party is being held. (Naturally, the aviators have nothing to do but drive a plane around the ground all day for Shirley.)

The biggest asset of the film, at least for modern audiences, is the redoubtable Jane Withers as the rich little brat who is Shirley's nemesis. Whether wailing outrageously because she didn't get a machine gun for Christmas, or wick-edly tormenting adorable "Miss Bright Eyes," Withers is a balm for the sticky fingers one feels developing after watching Shirley say her prayers at night and charm all those fly-boys by day.

Decked out in a gigantic hair ribbon and screwing up her face into cartoon-like anger, Withers can't help but get laughs when she informs the leading lady, "There ain't no Santa Claus because my psychiatrist says so." How many children secretly cheered her on while identifying with her realistic

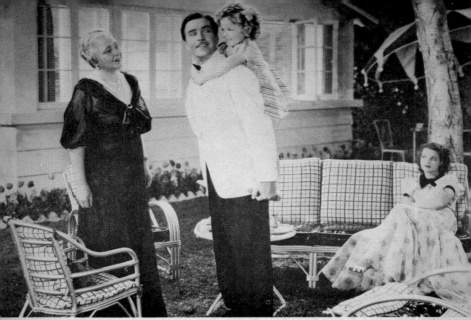

CURLY TOP (1935). With Esther Dale, John Boles, and Rochelle Hudson

anger and jealousy? Audience pleasure in Withers was enough to make her a top child star in her own right, second only to Temple for a period of time. (Her fame has even carried her forward into an adult career as a television "lady plumber" for a series of cleanser commercials.) It is possible, in fact, that she was just a little bit too appealing as a brat for her own good —she never again appeared in a film with Shirley Temple!

Bright Eyes had an exciting finale, involving a bumpy airplane ride in a storm and a daring escape by parachute, with Shirley clinging like confectionary sugar to James Dunn as he bails out. It was a film that cost $190,000 to make (some sources say only $106,000) and it made that much back within three weeks after its release. Late in 1934 it was announced that Shirley Temple was the number one box-office draw of the year. She had grinned, sobbed, wriggled, pouted, and tapped her way to the top of the ladder. In less than three years, at the ripe old age of six, Shirley had gone from the baby carriage to the portable dressing room. All in all, eight Shirley Temple films were released in 1934. This would have been a record number for the most seasoned star, but for a tot of barely six years, it was a feat of incredible concentration and hard work. One look at the cash register and down came the decree from the Fox top brass: from now on, in all her films, Shirley Temple was to appear in every scene possible. Or, as the ludicrous directive was worded (no doubt while someone hummed "On the Good Ship Lollipop" in the background): "The baby's hands should be on the tiller every inch of the way."

Shirley's first 1935 release, *The Little Colonel*, reflects the confidence Fox had in their little star. Lavishly mounted, with beautiful sets and costumes, it originally contained an expensive "pink" sequence photographed in Technicolor. The cast was first-rate: beautiful Evelyn Venable, handsome John Lodge, and veteran Lionel Barrymore as a bushy eyebrowed old curmudgeon. *The Little Colonel* was also notable for being

Shirley's first pairing with Bill Robinson. Their "dance duet" up a staircase, his big shoes and her little ones tap-tapping away in close-up, is one of the most memorable moments of thirties popular cinema. These two troupers also did a "copy-cat" tap routine that considerably livened up the pace of the otherwise predictable movie. It was a standard story in which Shirley, in a dripping-magnolias setting of a mythical Old South, acts as a catalyst in reuniting Barrymore with his estranged daughter (Venable, who played Shirley's mother) and his son-in-law, played by John Lodge.

The studio now became aware that, with a star like Shirley Temple, they were always working against time. She was, after all, a little girl whose every birthday brought her closer to a possible de-

THE LITTLE COLONEL (1935). With Lionel Barrymore

OUR LITTLE GIRL (1935). With Rosemary Ames and Joel McCrea

cline in screen popularity. *Our Little Girl*, her next film, reflects their philosophy of "rush-to-make-money" more than any other of her movies. It may be her worst film. With no musical numbers (except for a brief lullabye sung to her doll), a dull supporting cast, and a story that could be the definition of trite, *Our Little Girl* sputters along to a disjointed conclusion. It tells the story of a young doctor (Joel McCrea) who is too busy to spend time with his beautiful wife (Rosemary Ames) and daughter (Shirley Temple). He finally shows concern and even becomes angry and jealous when his bored, neglected wife starts horseback-riding with the rich playboy (Lyle Talbot) who conveniently lives next door. A divorce nearly takes place, but a kindly old tramp (J. Farrell Mac-Donald) saves the day by befriending the runaway Shirley and counseling the neglectful McCrea.

Our Little Girl is the flattest of soap operas, featuring pseudo-elegance for the lower classes: demitasse beside the fireplace, with the three principal adults in dinner clothes, making chi-chi conversation. Shirley Temple does her best to carry a screenplay that even Atlas couldn't move. The plot stops short every few minutes for the camera to linger on Shirley in loving close-up, doing her "stunts": testing a cake with a broom straw, playing "Oh, Susannah" on the piano with chubby hands, making her own picnic lunch, and teeter-tottering up and down, up and down, with her Scottie bravely holding down the opposite end. Naturally, this latter scene ends with Shirley's toppling off, providing the audience with its first glimpse of her fetching behind, rotundly encased in little underpanties. There is also the usual amount of daddy-hugging and straightforward talk from Shirley. As would become traditional, the film ends with a close-up of Shirley, smiling and bubbling and showing off the last of her many wardrobe changes. More than anything else, the incredible number of dresses she wears in *Our Little Girl* marks her as completely and utterly the *star*.

Curly Top, another enormous success, followed a Daddy Long Legs format, with a rich benefactor (John Boles) keeping his identity secret from the two young orphans he befriended, a cheerful Shirley and her older sister, Rochelle Hudson. The credits indicate where the box-office power lay: Shirley alone was billed over the title and it was her head of curls (fifty-five of them, by actual press-agent count) that was first seen on screen, followed by the turning of her head and a full fifty seconds of her sparkling smile and dimpling cheeks.

Shirley is at the top of her young form: taking her horse into bed with her on a rainy night; imitating the nasty old trustee of the orphanage who refuses to buy swings and sandboxes; and singing one of her

OUR LITTLE GIRL (1935).
With Rosemary Ames

biggest hits, "Animal Crackers in My Soup."

The script and dialogue of this film are excruciatingly banal. But Fox wasn't relying on dialogue to carry a Shirley Temple picture. Instead, there are long close-ups of the little star, in one of which she recites two childish poems without a single hesitation. And although Rochelle Hudson is a beautiful young actress, when Boles sings his romantic ballad ("It's All So New to Me"), it is Shirley Temple's face that is superimposed on all the paintings in the room.

CURLY TOP (1935). With John Boles

Arthur Treacher, in the first of four appearances with Shirley —allegedly his job was to entertain her on the set—gives strong support as the trusty butler, Reynolds. His snobbish utterance of his trademark, "Oh, my word!" is used as a comic counterpart to Temple's own oft-repeated "Oh, my goodness!"

Depression audiences were delighted with this escapist fare, as *Curly Top* provided a vicarious glimpse of the rich life. The hero's "little place at Southampton" is a world of all-white pianos, dinner with finger bowls, and "coffee on the terrace, please, Reynolds." Hudson and Temple sleep in an almost surreal bedroom fitted out in a nautical motif and stuffed with toys.

When the two former orphans, clad in silk pajamas, say good night and the lights go down, an eerie phalanx of large and expensive dolls stand guard around a ledge in the room, presumably to keep the wolf from the door. A montage showing Boles signing bills for expensive playthings stands as a tribute to trivial capitalism and wishful thinking that can equal the best the thirties has to offer. Aquaplane Board, $40.00; Pony Cart, $167.50; Hula Dance Costume, $45.00; and Ukulele, $8.00. Obviously, the ukulele was a bargain, especially since it gives an excuse to show little Shirley executing a suggestive hula at a late-evening beach picnic!

It is amazing that a film so ordinary in every respect could have

CURLY TOP (1935). With Rafaela Ottiano, Jane Darwell, Etienne Girardot, and John Boles

been such a huge success. The credit must go to Shirley Temple, for it is her clever playing which gives *Curly Top* any life and vigor it has. At the "charity bazaar" (the charity being mainly for the audience, who need more musical numbers from Shirley), Hudson feebly sings "Why Keep Reaching for the Moon" in a costume which makes her a dead ringer for Disney's Snow White. Shirley does an amazing tour de force to "When I Grow Up." She sings, dances, changes costume, and ages from a teenager to a bride to an old lady in a rocking chair, coming back on for a sensational finish with a fancy tap-and-jumping-rope routine. Later, she does one of her best tap numbers on top of the white piano while Boles sings the title song.

Why did audiences love this sentimental mush? Maybe it was a wish fulfillment of the sort the villainous head of Curly Top's orphanage (Rafaela Ottiano) expresses when she breaks down and weeps as Shirley and Hudson drive away in a ritzy car, wearing new dresses. "Why can't I be happy, too?" she sobs, and the cold breath of reality is suddenly present.

In June of 1935, Fox Films merged with 20th Century Pictures to form the 20th Century-Fox Film Corporation, the banner under which the rest of Shirley's seven-year contract was carried out. This merger brought about a shake-up of top personnel: Winfield Sheehan resigned as vice president and went over to Paramount. The new production head, Darryl F. Zanuck, inherited one fabulous asset among his new headaches and problems: Shirley Temple. At the star-studded banquet given to celebrate the deal, someone picked Shirley up in his arms. A horrified silence fell on the room as the combined bankers, business executives, producers, and moneylenders realized that the gentleman was holding all the assets of the company in his two hands. (Allegedly he was heard to say, "I was so scared I nearly dropped her" in one of those wonderful and no-doubt apocryphal stories of the halcyon studio days.)

Her next film, *The Littlest Rebel*, was the first to carry the wording "Darryl F. Zanuck in charge of Production." Similarities between the title of this film and her earlier *The Little Colonel* cause the films to be often confused. The additional similarity of having her dance with Bill Robinson in both adds to the problem. This later film is actually quite different in tone from the earlier production, and is on all counts a better movie. One of her best stories, handsomely photographed and well mounted, *The Littlest Rebel* has an element of suspense and excitement, notably a stirring night chase by Union soldiers.

THE LITTLEST REBEL (1935). With Bill Robinson

There is music, too, in Shirley's singing "Believe Me If All Those Endearing Young Charms" to "Daddy" John Boles and in dancing and singing to "Polly Wolly Doodle" with Robinson. Robinson also does a delightful, spirited tap to amuse the children at Shirley's lavish birthday party which opens the film. As usual, there is a dying mother to shed tears over and a regiment to charm, and Shirley steers a firm course through what was by then familiar territory for her.

The Littlest Rebel was an enormous hit, and contains a famous moment of real history crossed with *reel* history. The all-American miniature sweetheart meets with the all-American super-President, Abraham Lincoln. Here is Shirley taking her case—saving her Confederate officer father from the firing squad—to the highest court of them all, and, if not exactly straightening the President out, at least giving him some much-needed information. The sight of her golden curls snuggled up to Lincoln's hatchet face is a portrait of two American folk stars. Frank McGlynn, Sr., who plays Lincoln, looks so much like the sharp-featured Hoosier that the scene between them is eerie, but effectively handled, with a nice

THE LITTLEST REBEL (1935). With John Boles

CAPTAIN JANUARY (1936). With Buddy Ebsen.

touch of sassy humor involving their sharing of an apple. Shirley's refreshing smile and matter-of-fact acting style kept most of her potentially maudlin scenes from sliding too far into the chocolate sauce, and this big moment was no exception.

Next in line on the Temple parade of hits was *Captain January*. Based on a Laura E. Richards story, "The Lighthouse at Cape Tempest," it was the story of an orphaned tot saved from a shipwreck by the latest entry into Shirley's Museum of Melted Meanies. This time he was played by veteran character actor, Guy Kibbee. As usual, the plot really doesn't matter. What does matter is the number of Shirley's close-ups and songs, as well as the miniature capers she is allowed to cut. In this particular case, the number is quite high and *Captain January* accordingly ranks high on her list of films.

In particular, her wonderful dance with rag-doll Buddy Ebsen to the lively tune, "At the Codfish Ball," is a musical number of top quality. A "dancing" camera tracks along a country village wooden street, following Shirley and Buddy as they dance over rain barrels, stacked boxes, and up and down wooden stairs. Years ahead of the "down the streets" dance in *Cover Girl* which most film historians consider innovative, Shirley was mak-

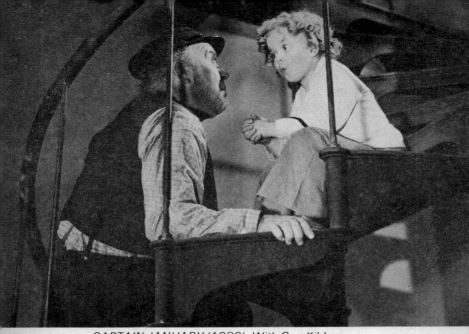

CAPTAIN JANUARY (1936). With Guy Kibbee

ing musical genre history! This number (choreographed by Jack Donohue) is probably her best overall song-and-dance routine on film, even better than her wonderful pairings with Bill Robinson. She is at the peak of her dancing ability, just before the steps and gestures became slightly too polished to be really charming.

Shirley follows her pattern of speaking in whatever jargon is appropriate to the setting of the film. Just as she said, "Merry Christmas, and plenty of tailwind" to the aviators in *Bright Eyes* and "Nix to that" to the Runyonesque bookmakers of *Little Miss Marker*, here she talks like an old sea salt: "I guess I'd better up anchor!" The rest of the salty dialogue is divided between Guy Kibbee and Slim Summerville, who conduct a love affair of traded insults ("clumsy old son of a sea slug" and "you blubberheaded blowfish"). One comic highlight has these two reliable old comedians pairing with Shirley in a hilarious send-up of grand opera.

Shirley, whose "Early Bird" number opens the film, plays with her most natural charm. Her voluptuous thighs encased in sailor's slacks, she giggles and winks and chuckles and dimples away until, finally and utterly, she is irresistible. Not to enjoy Shirley Temple in *Captain January*, a film of pleasant fluidity and great good humor, would require a deliberately perverse nature.

Her next film, *Poor Little Rich Girl*, reflected the public's increased awareness of what Shirley's private life was all about. Since it was now 1936, Shirley's name and face were everywhere, and she was the biggest box-office draw Fox had. This film fed the public's image of her own private life by opening with shots which establish Shirley as a rich girl beyond the audiences' wildest dreams. Her room contains dolls, dolls, dolls, including a set of five identical babies who are supposed to be the Dionne Quintuplets, that other childish economic phenomenon of the 1930's. Shirley has three dogs, a herd of ponies in the yard, rows of shoes in a closet, hundreds of little dresses, not to mention a maid, a butler, and a nurse—all to catch her every sneeze or sniffle. To make the poor moviegoing public feel better about all this affluence, Shirley sings wistfully, "I Want to Make Mud Pies (Then I Know I'd Find Happiness)."

Poor Little Rich Girl is the familiar story of the little girl with the too-busy father (Michael Whalen)—this time set against the back-

POOR LITTLE RICH GIRL (1936). With Jack Haley

ground of radio advertising in modern New York City. When her nanny is struck by a car while taking her away to boarding school, Shirley finds herself alone for the first time. She seizes the opportunity to take in a little of "the real life" and meets up with two hopeful radio performers, Alice Faye and Jack Haley. The now-standard ending for a Temple film has her straightening out both her father and his rival soap manufacturer (this month's candidate for Shirley's defrosted old-codger sweepstakes) and uniting her father with a brand-new wife (Gloria Stuart).

There are some lovely songs. Alice Faye does credit to "But Definitely" and "You've Got to Eat Your Spinach, Baby." Shirley sings "When I'm With You," a romantic ballad, to her own father in what must be one of the weirdest romantic scenes on record. (Over the years, many viewers complained about the undertones of Temple's pictures: a voluptuous little girl sitting in a grown man's lap and warbling about true love. In none of her pictures is this strange quality more present than *Poor Little Rich Girl*, in which she sings "marry me and let me be your wife" to her own father!)

POOR LITTLE RICH GIRL (1936). With Jack Haley and Alice Faye

DIMPLES (1936). With Frank Morgan and Billy Gilbert

Poor Little Rich Girl is a film fashioned out of nothing. Even the songs have to be stretched to fill in the gaps—Faye reprises Shirley's songs and Shirley reprises Faye's, etc. But even in such a flimsy film, audiences loved Shirley Temple. The final tacked-on number, "I Love a Military Man," was an obvious sop to fans who just wanted to see more of her. A tap number featuring Shirley, Faye, and Haley in military uniform, it was several weeks in rehearsal for Shirley to learn the intricate steps. Jack Haley recalled, "They dubbed in the taps of Shirley, but they didn't tell Mrs. Temple. They shot it with her, then they told

us to come back later and we did it again. And at the preview, her mother was boasting. 'Did you hear those taps? Could they have been any clearer? And you said Shirley couldn't do it!' " But whether or not Shirley tapped or didn't tap, the number was still hers—and so was the whole show! The little spotlight-stealer still knew her business.

But in *Dimples,* set in New York City in 1850, the inevitable finally happened: Shirley Temple met her match. For once, an adult stole the show from her. Frank Morgan, best remembered as the wonderful Wizard of Oz, plays Shirley's grand-

DIMPLES (1936). With Paul Stanton

father, "The Professor" (a cross between Mr. Micawber and Fagin)—a street thief who gives music lessons "in the pianoforte, the bugle, the mandolin, the drums . . . also bird calls." Spouting flowery language and never missing a chance to rip off a cuckoo clock here or a fur coat there, Morgan is one old curmudgeon who is beyond defrosting. The humor and energy of *Dimples*, as well as a large share of the footage, belong to him.

Shirley's performance as a street urchin who becomes a Broadway sensation in the first performance of "Uncle Tom's Cabin" (as Little Eva, of course) is competent, but lackluster. The original screenplay by Nunnally Johnson provides Shirley with ample musical exposure: she taps on street corners for pennies and warbles "He Was a Dandy and She Was a Belle" at a party for "rich swells." She does a tap audition for the part of Little Eva, and is seen performing to "Get On Board" during rehearsals for that show. But most of these numbers are short, or are cut into by action—something that hadn't happened to her since *Now and Forever*. Her big sit-in-lap-and-sing number is "When Somebody Loves Somebody" and, since it is Frank Morgan's lap, the director took no chances and photographed Morgan from the back of his head until near the end of the song. Finally, as if to apologize to the audience, Shirley has a chance to do her stuff in a pointless minstrel-show finale. "Dixie-ana, Oh Miss Dixie-ana, Come Out and Meet Me in the Moonlight" is delivered with her first signs of uncertainty and musical incompetence seen on screen. Her charm was still intact, but the movie was Frank Morgan's, and it is a credit to him that he was the only actor who could steal the show from 20th Century-Fox's Little Miss Moneybags!

Shirley's next was *Stowaway*. Once again, she was an orphan —this time the daughter of Chinese missionaries killed by bandits. Sent to Shanghai to escape further attacks, she is inadvertently hoisted on board a ship while asleep in the closed rumble seat of playboy Robert Young's roadster. While on board, she sparks a romance between Young and Alice Faye, thus saving Alice from a bad marriage

with a mother-dominated dullard. As if to make up for *Dimples*, all stops are pulled out for Shirley. The audience is treated to a barrage of her talents, as she speaks Chinese, plays Oriental musical instruments, dances and dimples away, quotes old Chinese proverbs at the drop of a joss stick, and even pushes credibility to the brink by imitating Al Jolson, Eddie Cantor, and, with a tuxedoed male doll attached to her toes, Fred Astaire and Ginger Rogers!

The music is particularly good: the lovely ballad long associated with Alice Faye, "Goodnight, My Love" (which is actually first sung by Shirley and later reprised less

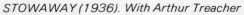

STOWAWAY (1936). With Arthur Treacher

WEE WILLIE WINKIE (1937). With C. Aubrey Smith

effectively by Faye); "You Gotta S-M-I-L-E" by Shirley; and "One Never Knows, Does One?" a really beautiful tune sung deliciously by Alice Faye in her languorous style. The finale has the young lovers together beside a gigantic Christmas tree, and Shirley warbling "That's What I Want for Christmas."

Next on the list was *Wee Willie Winkie*, directed by John Ford. Based loosely on Rudyard Kipling's story, originally written about a boy, *Wee Willie Winkie* is a child's adventure book come to life: an exotic locale, devilish Hindu villains, the pomp and circumstance of regimental life, and in the midst of it all and central to the adventure—the

young heroine.

Wee Willie Winkie was tailor-made for the Temple persona: a child with true grit not only saves the regiment but prevents a war. This time the men who get straightened out on important matters are wearing Scottish kilts or lavish turbans, but they still need Shirley to clear their heads for them. Shirley thaws out not one, but three tough masculine figures: the heathen leader, played by Cesar Romero; the official crusty old codger, her grandfather, regiment commander C. Aubrey Smith; and the comedy-relief, tough man Victor McLaglen as the sergeant who recruits her as "wee

58

Willie Winkie."

Wee Willie Winkie has a lively pace, authentic re-creation of locale, and exciting battle scenes. It is a superb adventure film, not without the gentle touches of visual storytelling for which John Ford is so justly famous. Unquestionably, it is one of Shirley Temple's best films. Although it can be classed as an *"auteur"* film by one of the great cinema masters, the audience knows from the first sight of Shirley, her beautiful wide-set eyes staring excitedly out a train window, that the film is mainly designed to satisfy her many fans. (This is particularly true of the edited versions which are shown on television, in which the majority of the action scenes are trimmed away.) Shirley's little tam-like hat has on its top a design of two concentric stars—lest the audience should forget!

A great deal of honest warmth (as compared to some of the more synthetic caloric content of other Temple films) is generated by the touching relationship between Victor McLaglen as the old soldier and Temple as his little recruit. Together they made an oddball Flagg and Quirt combination as they alternately bicker and affectionately tease each other. The famous scenes of Private Winkie, kilts bouncing, marching and drilling along with the adult soldiers, are still funny

WEE WILLIE WINKIE (1937). With Cesar Romero

and fresh today. Temple has told interviewers, "My favorite movie was *Wee Willie Winkie*. I marched, drilled, did the manual of arms, and had a wooden rifle. It was wonderful." Of John Ford she remarked, "Outwardly, he is a rugged person, but inside he's kindly and even sentimental."

The death of Victor McLaglen is a simple and beautiful moment. It is one of the few times that Shirley Temple was a child in an adult situation, instead of acting like a grown-up in a situation in which the adults were behaving like children. The beautiful photography by Arthur Miller bathes her in soft shadows as she comes to the hospital to visit her wounded friend. How small she looks as she presents her bouquet! Any possibility of too much sentiment is sharply cut by old-pro Ford's having her mischievously admit the flowers are stolen. When she stands by McLaglen's bed to sweetly sing "Auld Lang Syne," her singing is that of a small child who likes to sing and who knows a song rather than that of a billion-dollar baby star who tugs heartstrings as if they were pony reins. The camera remains on her shining face as she finishes, and McLaglen's hands droop slightly, loosening his grip on her flowers. The audience knows he is dead, but Shirley does not . . . . "Sh, he's asleep" . . . and she backs out, confident she has sung him to peaceful rest, as indeed she has. It is a moment of tender purity, and only the

WEE WILLIE WINKIE (1937). With Victor McLaglen

HEIDI (1937). With Jean Hersholt

most cynical could fail to appreciate its simple honesty. It stands out in a career of contrived emotional situations—although played by Temple as if it were the real thing—as the most sincere and truly child-like moment in all her films.

Much of the rest of *Wee Willie Winkie* draws on familiar Temple tricks: calmly peeling a banana, she sets out to negotiate a peace treaty with the villains. She coaxes C. Aubrey Smith into taking her mother to the regimental dance (a Ford trademark) by snuggling up to him while the sounds of Scottish folk songs are heard outside the win-

dows. ("You'd wheedle the whiskers off a thistle," complains Smith, but not without doing what she asks.)

Her next movie, *Heidi*, also directed by a veteran (Allan Dwan), was a natural for her. The Johanna Spyri classic of the plucky little Swiss girl seems almost to have been written with her in mind. She charms her reclusive old grandfather (Jean Hersholt in a superb performance), brings sunshine and light into a crippled girl's life, is menaced by a cruel old woman who tries to sell her to the gypsies, and settles the fates of the adults in a

HEIDI (1937). In the title role

straightforward manner.

Dwan's approach to this childhood classic is to modernize it, if not in sets and costumes, at least in attitude. He laces the syrupy story with pratfalls, high jinks, and such old tricks as a runaway monkey in a drawing room. He even lets a goat butt Shirley Temple in her famous rear end! Furthermore, the old-fashioned story is spiced up with a "dream sequence" in which, as Heidi's grandfather reads to her, the audience is taken into the storybook and allowed to see Shirley singing and dancing in Dutch costume. She also appears in lavish French revolutionary regalia, powdered wig and all, and dances a fancy minuet.

Heidi, one of her better films, illustrates the truth about Shirley Temple's stardom: she was not a child-actress who played it straight, but a child-star personality. Films were adjusted to her talents. She did not tackle a part and become the character—the character was remodeled into Shirley Temple.

Rebecca of Sunnybrook Farm, her film after *Heidi*, has practically nothing to do with the popular story by the same name.* Allan Dwan recalls, "I was able to say, 'Let's go after this with an update attitude—put some music in it —give Shirley something to sing—let's get radio in.' In fact when we were through, all we had

*Somewhat more faithful versions of the story had been filmed in 1917 (with Mary Pickford) and 1932 (with Marion Nixon).

REBECCA OF SUNNYBROOK FARM (1938). With Helen Westley

REBECCA OF SUNNYBROOK FARM (1938). With Bill Robinson

left was the title and the names of the characters." There could be no better description of the film. It's a mishmash of radio, old-fashioned storytelling, a few pratfalls, a few songs, and, like the meat in the stew, Shirley Temple performing like the old pro she now was. Her songs include "If I Had One Wish to Make" and "Come and Get Your Happiness." (There's also a lovely ballad, "Alone With You," sung by Jack Haley and Phyllis Brooks.) Any pretense at giving the audience anything other than their Shirley is thrown out the window. There's even a moment of blatant catering to her box-office power in which, as a newcomer making her radio debut, she sings and plays "some of

the songs I've introduced to you." The songs include "On the Good Ship Lollipop," "Animal Crackers," "When I'm with You," and "Goodnight My Love!" Seen in retrospect, this scene marks the last time that little girl Shirley sat down and sang her old favorites. It is her own farewell to childhood. By the time a similar reprise of the past occurred in *Young People,* film clips were used to evoke the ghost of the lost Shirley, as she herself could no longer generate the old magic.

Rebecca of Sunnybrook Farm is a pleasant enough film. Perhaps people fall down for laughs a bit more than necessary, but Dwan's handling of the pace is sure. Audiences evidently responded to its home-

LITTLE MISS BROADWAY (1938). With Donald Meek

LITTLE MISS BROADWAY (1938). With El Brendel and Jimmy Durante

spun message, which was, as one of its songs said, "in raggy britches there's a lot of riches." Certainly it was a message 20th Century-Fox wasn't going to argue with. The final number, reminiscent of Shirley's other "radio tap" (in *Poor Little Rich Girl*), is a military finale with Bill Robinson, performed to the "Parade of the Wooden Soldiers." Despite Haley's sour-grapes comment about her dubbed taps in the earlier number, her dancing here is snappy and attractive. The music is by turns martial, jazzy, and then a slow blues. Shirley, ably paired with Robinson, with whom she al-ways looked comfortable, is still at the top of her form.

Both *Rebecca of Sunnybrook Farm* and her next film, *Little Miss Broadway*, showed the public a somewhat plumper, slightly older-looking Shirley Temple. It was now 1938, and gone was the famous head of "curly top" corkscrew curls, as she sported a new and simpler hairdo. (And in case the public wanted to know what had happened, a line of dialogue was written into *Little Miss Broadway*: "I used to have curls all over my head," explains Shirley, "but they were a lot of trouble.")

Little Miss Broadway finds Shirley once again in the orphanage, but not for long. She is adopted and taken to the city by "Pops" (Edward Ellis), an ex-vaudevillian who used to know her parents. Pops now runs the Hotel Variety for out-of-work show people, but the hotel is threatened with foreclosure by its hard-hearted landlady, played by the marvelous, horse-faced Edna May Oliver. ("If you see a pumpkin in the window and it's not Halloween, that's our landlady.") Shirley and the hotel's inhabitants are befriended by Oliver's nephew (George Murphy), who does a beautifully mobile dance duet with Shirley to "We Should Be Together" (imaginatively choreo-graphed by Nick Castle and Geneva Sawyer). The bouncy tune provides a pleasant rhythm as they dance about the large foyer of Oliver's lavish home, hopping up on furniture, over tables, and around columns à la Fred Astaire and Ginger Rogers. Shirley had not had such a good dance created for her since her duets with Bill Robinson and the "Codfish Ball" number of *Captain January.*

Little Miss Broadway is most notable for its finale. Shirley pleads Murphy's case to a sour-faced judge (Claude Gillingwater) and says the show he wants to put on would be a success. "I want to see that show right here in this courtroom tomorrow," cries the judge—and sud-

JUST AROUND THE CORNER (1938). With Claude Gillingwater

THE LITTLE PRINCESS (1939). With Arthur Treacher

denly on comes the show, in a classically surreal presentation of two numbers: "Swing Me an Old-Fashioned Song" and "Little Miss Broadway." In the latter, Shirley rises up magically out of an all-white, totally unrealistic court-room chair, wearing a tiara and golden ballet slippers, and proceeds to twirl around the gigantic set with George Murphy (who, in top hat and tails, can't qualify even as a bush-league Fred Astaire). At the music's end, the two of them are tapping thunderously on the judge's bench, with illuminated pinwheels

gyrating wildly above his head. It was a production number of the sort Shirley seldom did: gigantic, improbable, and full of that madness that qualifies a musical number to be dubbed "pure thirties." In this case, her end close-up of "Oh, my goodness!" hardly does justice!

With *Little Miss Broadway* (and the film which followed, *Just Around the Corner*), her box office began to slip. "It can't be old age," said *The New York Times*, "but it does look like weariness." In fact, *Little Miss Broadway* would be one of Shirley's more forgotten vehicles except for a late sixties off-Broadway musical called *Curley McDimple*. This little show, done on a shoe-string on a tiny stage with a company of six actors, managed to become something of a minor theatrical miracle. A sellout for over two years, it was a satire on *Little Miss Broadway:* a rags-to-riches back-stage saga about a Broadway theatrical boarding house.

Just Around the Corner was what its title indicates: escapist enter-tainment. Shirley plays a rich man's daughter who is called home from her ritzy boarding school to find strangers living in their penthouse and her father down in the base-ment as house electrician. As usual, she faces this economic disaster with sunny equanimity and plunges into cooking, cleaning, and dispens-ing wisdom apparently gleaned from the *Child's Home Companion:*

"A man without a woman around the house is quite a problem" and "I have a man to take care of—you know how much trouble they can be!"

Between trips to the garbage pail, she finds time to sing and dance with Bert Lahr, Joan Davis, and Bill Robinson to "This Is a Happy Little Ditty." With these veterans— and also Franklin Pangborn, Charles Farrell, Cora Witherspoon, and Claude Gillingwater helping out—this portion of the film has pace and is pleasantly humorous. Shirley is relaxed, self-confident, and seems as bright and bouncy as ever.

However, when the plot compli-cations involve Shirley's mistaking a nasty old man (another one!) for America's Uncle Sam, things begin to go downhill. The promise of the earlier portion of the movie is not

THE LITTLE PRINCESS (1939). With Sybil Jason and Mary Nash

met by the second half, and one sits waiting for the problems to be ironed out and the final number to be rolled on.

It turns out to be worth waiting for, as it has Bill Robinson and Shirley singing and dancing to "I Love to Walk in the Rain." The set utilizes a charming lane with tulips, giant mushrooms, winsome bunnies, and the whole imaginary world of make-believe associated with Shirley Temple. The song barely finishes before a split-second wind-up has Shirley's father (an architect) hired to build a large slum project, his love interest settled, and the old devil "Uncle Sam" beaming fondly at the star. If the public could just hold on, the film suggested, prosperity was just around the corner. Unfortunately, most of the entertainment value of this film was further around the corner and out of sight. For non-fans of Shirley Temple, however, it does have one golden moment in which the perfect little child behaves more like Jane Withers. Mowing down a line of playmates with a toy machine gun, she spits out, "I guess that'll teach you a lesson. You can't fool a G-woman."

In *The Little Princess,* Shirley was back in familiar territory: a lavish costume movie with Dickensian overtones, based on the Frances Hodgson Burnett novel previously filmed in 1917 with America's earlier "sweetheart," Mary Pickford. Shirley's first Technicolor production, this handsomely mounted film took place in England in 1899, just in time for her daddy to march off to the Boer War. (Mother was again conveniently buried.) Although highly Victorian in content, it is just the sort of film Shirley's fans expected and wanted to see. It has the standard ingredients: a romantic young couple (attractively played by Anita Louise and Richard Greene), a tough old codger, a mean villainess, and a lovable comedy second-lead who can sing and dance with Shirley (Arthur Treacher). Its strong storyline provides Shirley with good comedy moments (dumping a load of fireplace ashes on two snobbish girls) and moments of pathos (bravely reciting "My daddy has to go away" as her father marches off to war). There is also heart-tugging suspense as Shirley narrowly misses her father while searching for him among the wounded at a hospital. Having had so much success with Lincoln in *The Littlest Rebel,* Fox dredged up that British romantic authority figure, Queen Victoria, to help Shirley settle her problems this time.

Because of its lavish production and well-constructed plot, *The Little Princess* was a critical success, but did not fare as well at the box office as another picture for children made the same year, *The Wizard of Oz*. A comparison of the two films indicates that the day of the sentimental Temple Valentine was perhaps drawing to a close, as a more modern and upbeat kind of fantasy took over and a less perfectly dimpled and curled child began her own tug on American heartstrings (Judy Garland). Ironically, Shirley Temple had originally been considered for *The Wizard of Oz* around 1937. Rumors even said her co-star would be W. C. Fields as the Wizard! (As Fields himself might say, the combination "boggles the mind.")

Many fans consider *The Little Princess* to be Shirley Temple's best overall picture. Certainly the beautiful Technicolor does much to enhance this film, and the charming musical production number (actually a miniature opera) which is presented as Shirley's "dream" gives her a chance to sing and dance in tutu and slippers. The basic theme of the story—from riches to rags —seemed to please the fans, who by now wanted to possess their little girl as "one of them." Some of the mechanical quality which had crept into Shirley's work in *Little Miss Broadway* and earlier films is nowhere here apparent. Her character is spunky and tenderhearted by equal turns, and the additional plus of the big production number (as

SUSANNAH OF THE MOUNTIES (1939). With Randolph Scott

SUSANNAH OF THE MOUNTIES (1939). With Randolph Scott and Moroni Olsen

well as her charming dance routine with Treacher to "Old Kent Road") provided much enjoyment to her fans.

Though the film was popular with audiences, it was really Shirley's swan song. It was her last great success as the world's most famous child star . . . and she would never again equal it while a youngster. But as the end to an extraordinary career, *The Little Princess* was a more than satisfactory "good-bye."

Susannah of the Mounties was Shirley's last film before her decline. Originally photographed in Sepiatone, it was a banal film in which the seeds of her destruction were all too apparent. Now too old for her dimpled face and pseudo-adult delivery to be unique, Shirley had to draw on any real talent she might have to make the picture move. It was no longer enough for her to waggle her finger in an adult's nose and deliver a little sermon which somehow seemed clever and funny just because it was coming from a child.

Susannah is the story of a little girl, the sole survivor of a wagon-train massacre, who is "adopted" by Canadian Mounties. As usual, there is an adult romance of sorts, this time between Randolph Scott and Margaret Lockwood, and an adult comedy-lead, an Irish aide-de-camp played by J. Farrell MacDonald. The plot, a contrived affair, is about Indians stealing horses from the railroad, and the railroad retaliating, with the Mounties obliged to settle it all.

The main interest lies in what is happening to Fox's big-time movie star, Miss Shirley Temple. Shirley was now eleven years old, and at the brink of her pre-adolescence. Apparently trying to capitalize on this, the studio allowed her role to vary somewhat from the usual formula. This time, there is a childish "romantic" interest (Martin Good Rider, the young son of an Indian chief) and an adult "romantic" interest who is not her own father (Scott, whose character name of Montie qualifies him for the laugh of the year as Montie the Mountie). Shirley is even allowed to pass the peace pipe, and is seen smoking it, not once, but three different times!

Shirley as Susannah (also known as Golden Hawk, Little Spirit of the Sun) is not in control of the situation for the first time. As the Little Chief's "squaw," she is not only pushed around but made to both walk and ride behind him. It is the great American tradition of the uppity woman getting just what she deserves from "her man"—Shirley's first battle of the sexes. Shirley is not without her own resources in the situation, however. Also in the great American tradition, she nags the Little Chief and sets the rules for his proper social behavior.

Shirley does have a few chances to repeat her familiar routines. She is given one small song and dance ("I'll Teach You to Waltz") and there is that inevitable moment when she and Scott cozy-up for a heart-to-heart conversation about life. Significantly, she does *not* sit on his lap, now being too large to keep such a scene from being ridiculous. The finale finds Shirley breaking up the Indian pow-wow and asking to speak to Mr. Big Eagle for all the world as if he were just another of those Depression judges or business tycoons who needed her counsel. The fact that, in this case, Mr. Big Eagle is preparing to roast Randolph Scott at the stake hardly seems to matter.

This was the last Shirley Temple film under her seven-year contract at Fox to make money. It is also one of her first really unpleasant characterizations. Susannah is a bossy "little wife" who, unlike her counterpart in *Just Around the Corner*, fails to win our hearts with her womanly ways. As she rearranges drawers, exhibits the worst kind of female jealousy toward Margaret Lockwood, and barks orders on how to make a bed properly, the viewer's patience is finally tried. When the

Indians say of her, "Devil Child speak with forked tongue," the audience feels like cheering. For the first time in her career, Shirley Temple fails to rise above her material. The mannerisms have become mechanical and the acting is now overblown, and without innocence. By the end of 1939, the handwriting was on the birthday cake.

Finally, the inevitable happened. Twelve-year-old Shirley Temple had her first flop. Not only was the 1940 *Blue Bird*, based on the play by Maurice Maeterlinck, a flop—it was a resounding financial disaster. The reasons are many: first of all, Shirley plays a spoiled brat, and although she reforms during the course of the movie, it is likely that her fans resented going to see Shirley Temple and being given Jane Withers instead. Secondly, its theme, although delicately handled in the film, is perhaps too sentimental for the general audience. *The Blue Bird* was directed by Walter Lang, and, as film historian William K. Everson points out, "Lang was never much more than a journeyman and adds little to the film that wasn't there when he walked onto the set." Under his direction, sections of the film have a curiously stagey quality, with long pauses between sentences, which is particularly jarring when set against the excellent special effects.

The Blue Bird is a fantasy without

THE BLUE BIRD (1940). With Johnny Russell, Russell Hicks, and Spring Byington

THE BLUE BIRD (1940). With Gale Sondergaard, Johnny Russell, and Eddie Collins

the bravura "show biz" approach of *The Wizard of Oz*, and its gentle, low-key quality no doubt harmed it as it was compared in audiences' minds with the earlier film. Additionally, its whimsy and fantasy are introduced to an unsuspecting audience suddenly after a long, detailed opening section (also like *Oz*, photographed in sepia) whereas *Oz* suggested the approaching fantasy even in its opening, non-color section by having Garland sing the haunting "Over the Rainbow." As entertainment, it has a slightly funereal quality, dealing with dead grandparents and unborn children.

For all of its shortcomings, *The Blue Bird* is an interesting film, and when it was revived at the San Francisco Film Festival in 1965 (with Temple in attendance), it was a huge success. It has enormous visual charm, a lovely song done sweetly by Temple ("Laddy-O"), and plenty of spectacular sets. The Land of Luxury is pure Hollywood Baroque: milk-white staircases edged in gold, blood-red carpets, and a pink-and-white merry-go-round set up in the foyer. There are other compensations for the adult audience. The actress who plays Light, for instance, a long-tressed blonde with a full bosom, wears a see-through white dress, and looks as if she should be playing Sex, not Light.

The strength of the film is in its special effects: characters jump magically into the air, animals turn into humans, and there is a spectacular, genuinely frightening fire in the forest. (Perhaps it is too frightening for most small Temple fans.) But Shirley herself is a problem. Her pouting little mouth, so provocative when she was a tiny tot, here begins to look petulant. Now that famous "kissing mouth" suddenly seems to reveal tension, or her own sense of "play-acting." Shirley is curiously languid. There isn't enough of her to satisfy fans and too much of her to please non-fans. Despite its superb production and dramatic special effects, *The Blue Bird* falls between the chairs in its appeal.

For her next film, Fox tried to steer Shirley back onto familiar territory. *Young People* was the usual Temple format about an orphan: a little baby is passed up over the footlights in a basket to a vaudeville couple who decide to raise her as their own. The film even makes a noble effort to evoke the ghost of

YOUNG PEOPLE (1940). With Jack Oakie

Shirley's past by using clips from her previous films: "Baby, Take a Bow" from *Stand Up and Cheer* and the hula dance from *Curly Top*. There was also a brand-new number with her co-stars, Jack Oakie and Charlotte Greenwood: "Strolling on Fifth Avenue." But Shirley Temple, at age twelve, is a dead legend. Suddenly it's as if the magic has gone out of her. The voice is slight, the dancing is adequate, but just adequate, and there is a mechanical "best pupil at the local dance recital" quality to her work. She is now old enough to be judged as a performer, not as a remarkable little child. Sadly, she fails the test.

There is something disquieting in the adolescent Shirley Temple. The perfection of her features, so lovely when she was little, suddenly seems *too* perfect. The golden curls, the careful diction, the round, smooth face—all are too much. One suddenly longs for an awkwardness —freckles, a lost tooth, a knobby knee—something, anything, to make her human! A cuddly kitten has suddenly turned into a musical robot.

Young People marks the end of Shirley Temple's childhood career. Ironically, it is a film about the passing of time and the inevitable changes it brings. A little girl has grown up and become just like other little girls.

Fox tries hard with *Young People*. Director Allan Dwan's pace has a pleasing fluidity, particularly in the opening scenes. Besides "Strolling on Fifth Avenue" and the clips from her earlier successes, Shirley sings "I Wouldn't Take a Million Dollars for a Mom and Dad Like You" and "Tra La La La La." There is humor (of the villainess, she says, "She must have been weaned on a pickle"), and a wicked little girl who appears at a dramatic moment to reveal that Shirley is adopted. There is even a hurricane—but nothing helps.

Near the end of the film, Shirley and a group of peers sing, "We're not little babies anymore. . . . We know how to act our age. . . . We think children are an awful bore. . . . We're young people." But looking at their unformed bodies and their inexperienced faces, the audiences feel a sense of gloom. For one grim moment at the end of her childhood, Shirley is right back where she started—in the Baby Burlesks.

YOUNG PEOPLE (1940). With Arleen Whelan

I stopped believing in Santa Claus at an early age. Mother took me to see him in a Hollywood department store, and he asked me for my autograph.

Shirley Temple

RICH LITTLE RICH GIRL

When Shirley Temple finished what turned out to be her last picture at Fox (the unpopular *Young People*), less than six years had passed since *Stand Up and Cheer*. In that time, she had made twenty-four feature films and had chalked up profits of more than twenty-five million dollars for the studio. She had become not only a star but also that dream of all American fame-seekers, "a household word." An unknown in 1933, she had placed among the top ten box-office stars in 1934, along with Will Rogers, Clark Gable, Joan Crawford, and others. By 1935, she was at the head of the list, having outranked not only Will Rogers, Gable, and Crawford, but also Astaire and Rogers, Cagney, Colbert, and every other movie star in Hollywood's heavens. She continued as the number-one box-office attraction throughout 1936, 1937, 1938, and she was among the top ten for 1939—a record seldom equaled. By the time she was six years old, she had unquestionably earned her right to the Hollywood Hall of Lasting Fame.

It's one thing to be a top movie star—it's quite another to be a top movie star who is also a child. During the years 1934 to 1940, while Shirley Temple doubled her age, millions of people dreamed of having a child just like her—and millions of others tried to turn their own children into carbon copies. When she was translated into strips of celluloid and shipped in cans from Walla Walla to Winnetonka, she became a national commodity, like Lux Soap or Coca-Cola. Shirley Temple was an economic spur (whether by direct endorsement or casual association) for everything from soap to dresses to toys. Her name was such a powerful merchandising tool that it was estimated the Temple family took in over $10,000 in assets from its use in any given ten-day period. She also became an object of public adulation, receiving gifts, honors, awards, 3,500 fan letters per week, and over $300,000 per year in salary . . . not to mention the anger, hate, and jealousy of millions of crackpots. Her story, the fairy tale of a little girl movie star, reads like a true American myth. It was a three-ring circus that could only happen on the Hollywood back-lot, a chain of events that was cultural madness.

At a "Mother Goose" party in 1936

First there was the "Shirley Temple Permanent," guaranteed to turn even the most stubbornly straight little-girl hair into a riotous mass of curls which, if not golden, were at least genuinely corkscrewed. (As for the non-golden part, there was something to handle that, too: "Baby peroxide for the little miss, the gentlest of lighteners" . . . probably guaranteed to turn the baby back to its birthday baldness!)

Next there were Shirley Temple dresses. Mrs. Temple had promised that every single design which bore the Temple name would actually have been on Shirley's body for a trial run. (Nobody bothered to figure out just how many times she would have had to change her dress daily to accomplish this.)

Soon came the toys and playthings. The Ideal Novelty and Toy Company placed its first ad (in the October 1934 issue of *Playthings Magazine),* announcing The Shirley Temple Doll, "made in exact likeness of that now famous young movie star who has become the darling of the screen."

Throughout the next six years, these dolls, of various shapes and sizes and wearing different costumes, were to be a mainstay of Ideal toy production, allegedly saving the company from bankruptcy. There were 27-inch dolls and

18-inch dolls. Dolls in red-and-white plaid and dolls in the *Curly Top* knife-pleated dress. There was a "baby Shirley at age two" doll, and a smaller (and thereby cheaper) doll which "reproduced with photographic fidelity Shirley's winning smile, laughing eyes, cute dimple, and hair." What's more, it reproduced all these adorable features in time for Christmas, and at a new lower price that even the masses could afford. The sales from these dolls were so enormous that, in the early years, before her salary increases, they brought the Temple family more money than Shirley's film work. Ideal was forced to move its headquarters to a bigger building to cope with the sales, as well as to think up new variations.

One of the most elaborate of these ideas was an early doll called "the little colonel specialty"— elegantly attired in pink organdy and wearing a beautiful old-fashioned hat with a contrasting plume and bow (also available in pink, yellow, lavender, and green silk!). Little girls who liked to travel could coax their parents to buy "the

With a Shirley Temple doll

*A Shirley Temple paper doll book
(Photo courtesy of
Loraine Burdick)*

Besides the Ideal Shirley Temple dolls, there were figures, figurines, and "standees"—a combination of paper and cardboard made to stand alone as a Shirley outline figure for merchandising purposes. And, of course, well within the poorest fan's price range—the paper dolls. These inexpensive sets included such variations as Shirley with costumes from all her films (available in both snap-on and magnetic dresses), with her playhouse, in masquerade costumes, and later on in teen-age dresses.

Nor did it end with dolls. By the time the merchandising of Shirley Temple products began to move into full swing, her name was so well-known it was claimed she could have sold horse manure (for the child's garden of verses?). There were Shirley Temple book ends, and bars of soap carved in the shape of Shirley dressed for her "Baby, Take a Bow" number in *Stand Up and Cheer*. There were playhouses, including one design made in several sizes with seven-foot walls and a large porch (selling for eighty-five dollars and up and suggesting that the home-grown variety of Shirley Temples had better find themselves a rich old lady or man to defrost). Little girls could wear Shirley Temple lockets and charm bracelets, and little boys could have Shirley Temple watches with a snappy masculine strap. There were comic

trunk set," which had a Shirley doll that fit inside a little steamer trunk and had clothes on small hangers, with shoes and stockings tucked away in miniature drawers. For the hard-to-please there was a cowgirl Shirley . . . or a Wee Willie Winkie doll . . . and, naturally, a Heidi doll. There were official doll carriages and unofficial doll furniture, and Shirley patterns for Mamas who wanted to sew their own doll clothes.

Shirley Temple sheet music: "How Can I Thank You" from LITTLE MISS BROADWAY, and "On Account-a I Love You," one of her first music sheets. (Photo courtesy of Loraine Burdick)

books, coloring books, sheet music, records, big little books and little big books (even in foreign-language editions). There was the ever-popular Shirley Temple mug—available only by buying a box of Bisquick—and a cream pitcher that came with the purchase of two packages of Wheaties. (Offer limited to one cream pitcher to a family, please!) Contests of all kinds used Shirley as a come-on: win a prize by painting a doll to look like her . . . draw her face . . . design a dress for her. It was a never-ending parade.

Since any knowledge that the Little Wonder owned a certain doll or toy naturally spurred sales of that item, manufacturers sent her "samples" of their wares to keep. Shirley posed for pictures with some of these toys and used others in her pictures. Raggedy Ann and Andy dolls, tiny china tea sets, elegant Princess dolls, jointed wooden Popeyes, hand-painted alphabet blocks, stuffed ducks with signs that

At the piano in her studio bungalow

said "Joe Penner,"* kilted Scottish dolls, four-poster doll beds with canopies, large colorful drums, little red wagons, oversized stuffed rabbits and bears . . . and more, much more. On her "eighth" birthday, she received over 135,000 gifts from fans, including a baby kangaroo, a fancy leather saddle, and a Jersey calf.

Early in 1934, Shirley began to acquire her own remarkable doll collection, which is still leased to museums on a yearly basis. Some of her favorites were a beautiful blonde doll brought from Denmark by Winfield Sheehan, and a china lady from Germany, exquisitely dressed in lace and velvet. There were Spanish dolls and Finnish dolls, and Oriental dolls in kimonos and obis, and a set of early Disney dolls. Fans sent her a miniature set of dolls from the Japanese Girls' Doll Festival, and she had her own set of the five matching little Dionne Quintuplet dolls which were used in *Poor Little Rich Girl*.

Besides her dolls, Shirley, al-

*Joe Penner was a thirties comedian whose trademark question was, "Wanna buy a duck?".

legedly something of a tomboy, played at home with a sample Roy Rogers flare gun, some G-man artillery, cap pistols, and an air rifle ("That was quickly taken away from me," she reported). Her favorite radio show at this time was "Gang Busters." She also had her own pony (Spunky, named for her horse in *Curly Top*), and two dogs, Corky (a Scottie) and Rowdy (a cocker spaniel). Later she acquired a Pekingese, called Ching-Ching after her nickname in *Stowaway*. She had a small pool-going sloop named *Safe and Sound* (a gift from songwriters Mack Gordon and Harry Revel) and a gasoline-powered little car with her name on the side, with a maximum speed of five miles per hour (a gift from Bill Robinson). Set behind the Temple house was her famous playhouse, which had its own stage, projection room, obligatory soda fountain, and even a little "pretend store" with tiny scales, wrapping paper, and shelves stocked with candy.

At the studio, a special ordinance allowed her to keep chickens and raise rabbits on the lot. She naturally had her own gorgeous dressing

With co-Oscar winner, Claudette Colbert, 1934

room complete with a marvelous doll house from a 1935 Fox film in which she had not even appeared (*Orchids to You*). This tiny house, which Shirley adored, featured miniature "grounds" with small trees, a picket fence, and sunflowers and roses growing in its "yard." Inside, there were tiny hooked rugs, magazine racks with real magazines, tiny goblets and pitchers, and a desk with an incredibly small quill pen that had its own real ink. There were little books in all the bookcases, curtains at every window—everything, right down to a fashionable metal peacock to sit on the sideboard.

It wasn't all toys, however. Shirley Temple also received the world's honors, one after another in overwhelming tribute. She was Captain of the Texas Rangers, an Honorary Chairman of Be-Kind-to-Animals anniversary week, and a Kentucky Colonel. She was Honorary Captain of the Waikiki Beach Patrol with her own special surfboard which said *Aloha Captain Shirley*. She was President of the Chums Club in Scotland and of the Kiddies Club in England. Osa Johnson shot a spotted leopard for her, and Congress called her "the most beloved individual in the world." J. Edgar Hoover made her an Honorary G-Man, and the American Legion made her its youngest Honorary Sponsor of National Airmail Week. Topping them all, President Arturo Alessandri of Chile, a Temple fan who called her Rocito di Oro (Golden Curls), had her officially named mascot to the Chilean Navy, a dignity which included her very own special uniform. She led the Rose Bowl Parade and sang "Happy Birthday" to President Roosevelt (while sitting on his lap, of course). And the world's bartenders immortalized her in their own way with the "Shirley Temple"—a drop of grenadine in a glass of ginger ale—garnished with a maraschino cherry. In short, she was the recipient of everything but an honorary college degree—an oversight which, under the circumstances, can be forgiven.

Naturally the movie industry itself was not left behind. In recognition of her phenomenal rise to stardom (not to mention her phenomenal effect on the box office), the Motion Picture Academy of Arts and Sciences awarded her a special "Oscar" at the end of 1934. The citation read. "There was one great towering figure in the cinema game in 1934, one artiste among artists, one giant among troupers. The award is bestowed because Shirley Temple brought more happiness to millions of children and millions of grown-ups than any other child of her years in the history of the world." The evening's master of ceremonies, humorist Irvin S.

At the Grauman's Chinese Theatre ceremonies, 1935, with Robert T. Smith, the manager, and Sid Grauman

Cobb, presented Shirley with her award in front of more than nine hundred guests at the Biltmore Bowl on the night of February 27, 1935. Legend says that she had to be waked up to receive it, but she was awake enough to pose for pictures with Cobb and best actress of the year, Claudette Colbert. In presenting the award, Cobb sentimentalized, "When Santa Claus brought you down creation's chimney, he brought the loveliest Christmas present that has ever been given to the world."

In March of 1935, Shirley literally cemented her position in Hollywood's elite by placing her handprints and footprints in the sidewalk area in front of Grauman's Chinese Theatre—the official recognition of "star arrival" in the hard-bitten commercial world. Shirley wrote her own message— "Love to you all'—in a childish scrawl.

By 1937 her yearly income was placed at $307,014, making her the seventh-highest-paid person in the United States. She was so much a Hollywood legend that she was used as the perfect joke for a film about Hollywood, *Stand-In*, directed by Tay Garnett and starring Leslie Howard, Joan Blondell, and Humphrey Bogart. Blondell played a former child-star, "the Shirley Temple of my day," and Howard was characterized as so out of it he "doesn't even know who Shirley Temple is." There was also a scathing satire of a child-star as Howard is attacked by a stage mother dragging a little tot. Mama whips a harmonica out of her purse and barks, "Hit it, kid!" to her daughter, and the little girl bumps and grinds into a mock-Temple rendition of "Is It True What They Say About Dixie?" As little "Elvira" wiggles her bottom suggestively in front of Howard (with Mama yelling, "Do that Mae West number" in the background), the beleaguered man cries, "Leave at once or I'll be forced to call the juvenile authorities." As if this weren't enough, Blondell does a really mean (but funny) imitation of Shirley singing "On the Good Ship Lollipop." (Of course, Temple had her very own stand-in—originally it had been little Marilyn Granas, but Mary Lou Islieb had taken over during the filming of *Baby, Take a Bow* and the two little look-alikes remained lifetime friends.)

But *Stand-In*'s satire notwithstanding, most of the world just couldn't praise her enough. *Variety* called her "a cinch female Jackie Cooper and Jackie Coogan rolled into one." On the set, she was known as "one-take" Shirley because of her uncanny ability to memorize lines—hers and other people's—and get them right in the first take. Darryl Zanuck described

On the set of DAVID HARUM with Will Rogers

her, "She's the eighth wonder. If I told her to ice skate for a picture, she'd probably be doing all of Sonja Henie's tricks within a couple of days." Director David Butler (who worked with her on several films) remarked, "She doesn't act or make pictures. She plays wonderful games. Why . . . even her baby teeth fall out between pictures . . . that's how good her timing is!"

Her little bungalow was visited by a steady stream of adoring celebrities whose only wish, publicity seemed to indicate, was to sit at the Mary-Janes of this diminutive movie star. They all came—Harry Lauder and General Pershing, Al Smith and H.G. Wells. Eleanor Roosevelt, who, after all, went everywhere, came, as did J. Edgar Hoover, Henry Morgenthau, Bernarr MacFadden, and novelist Thomas Mann. Even cynical Noël Coward came, and proudly wore his Shirley Temple police badge.

The praise of her co-stars, many of whom had their scenes stolen right out from under them, also seemed unending. Lionel Barrymore remarked that, "Talent drips from her fingertips. She has an extraordinary instinct for acting, a real naturalness." Bill Robinson called her "the sweetest little peach-blow lady in the world. Uncle Bill doesn't tell her feet where to go, her heart, it tells her."

Others who worked with her, more honest, perhaps, and certainly more realistic, faced the moppet and blanched. "God! Where does she get all that pep?" moaned George Murphy on the set of *Little Miss Broadway*. And perhaps most honest of all, when faced with her uncanny ability to snuggle in just close enough so that *his* face fell in the shadow, Adolphe Menjou stated flatly on the set of *Little Miss Marker*, "I want to quit."

Almost anything about Shirley Temple made news—magazines could devote an entire article to telling their readers that her hair was actually dull gold, not yellow, or that her eyes were hazel, not blue. She appeared in an average of twenty still portraits daily in the nation's newspapers and magazines. Publicity men went crazy reporting the day that word was sent down to production-head Darryl Zanuck that she had lost a front tooth. (Zanuck, in conference with an important novelist, supposedly shouted, "Her *front* tooth? For God's sake, get the best dentist . . . and close down the studio!")

There were stories on Shirley's genius IQ, and her remarkable instant memory for lines and tap routines. One magazine carried a story on how Shirley wanted to play with the Dionne Quintuplets "as a Christmas present" and another called her "a miracle star that only comes along once in a decade." (Ac-

With her two brothers, Jack and George

tually, a decade was a highly conservative estimate!) Interviewers recorded her every quote. When she was introduced to H. G. Wells and was told he was the most important man in the universe, she chirped "Oh, no he's not. God is the most important and the Governor is second." *Time Magazine* put her on their cover and remarked about how, unlike most film stars, Shirley "does not conceal the date of her birth." (The joke was on *Time*, since Shirley's true age had not yet been revealed.)

With all this going on around them, what happened to the quiet-living George Temple family

of Santa Monica? They hung on in the whirlwind gamely, trying their best to create an atmosphere of modesty and calm around their little gold mine. One potential problem, sibling rivalry, was more or less eliminated by the differences in age between Shirley and her older brothers. When Jack and George got fed up with Shirley, they called her La Temple and let it go at that. They seemed to delight in her success, which afforded them an indirect access to the limelight also.

At first, the Temples tried to live on in their old neighborhood, but later they moved to larger quarters and still later to an estate in Brentwood, a beautiful residential area of Los Angeles. Mr. Temple finally left his position at the bank to manage Shirley's finances. As his daughter had become more and more successful, Mr. Temple's working in a public place had created problems. "Daddy left the bank by mutual consent after I became *notorious*," Temple said later. "Mothers used to bring their children in to tap in front of him and sing in off-key voices." There were other problems, too—determined women who thought, with just a little help from Mr. Temple, they, too, could produce a Shirley Temple. Their overt offers were an embarrassment to both the bank and Mr. Temple (who was short, plump, and dimpled, and looked a great deal like Shirley).

As Shirley's financial manager, Mr. Temple put his banking experience to good use. Her money was invested soundly in government bonds, annuities with old-line insurance companies, and trust funds.

During this period, the main question most of the movie-going public wanted to know was—was the kid a brat or not? Was she hopelessly spoiled and rotten behind the scenes? Was there a Mistress Hyde?

Apparently not. According to practically everyone who knew Shirley then, or who worked with her, the little girl was a peewee paragon who not only obeyed her mother in all matters, but even took her daily dose of castor oil willingly! To the little movie star that the world just couldn't find enough awards for, a real honor was a gold star she received when she excelled in her lessons.

Shirley Temple appeared to be a healthy and normal little girl who took stardom in stride. After all, she knew no other life—to her it was the way things were. The famous people who trooped through her bungalow were merely "visitors" to her. She lost interest in General Pershing when she heard he didn't know any movie stars, and asked him how, if that were so, he had become a general. Between takes, she played happily in her "doll house" bungalow, swinging in her special swings and digging in the sand which had been carefully laid around the house for her. ("If only I'd dug deeper," she was to comment years later, "I might have struck oil.") She loved corny jokes and liked to play riddles with Bill Robinson, with whom she also did old-fashioned vaudeville routines. Robinson would feed her the line, "How's the tailoring business?" "So-so," she'd reply. Mrs. Temple taught her to be self-reliant and saw to it that she was kept as protected as possible from the adulation of fans.

On the dark side of Shirley's success and adulation were actual phys-

Sailing to Bermuda with her mother and father, 1938

ical dangers: over-zealous fans who frightened her by tearing her clothes and pulling her little curls, or threats of kidnapping which brought the head of the FBI, J. Edgar Hoover, personally out to Hollywood to set up security precautions, including six-foot walls, electrified gates, barred windows, electric eyes wired to police alarms, and chauffeurs with pistols. Frustrated stage mothers whose little ones weren't getting the breaks Mommy thought they deserved made pathetic threats. One mother said she would throw acid in Shirley's face, and another tried to mail her a box of poisoned candy.

20th Century-Fox took no chances and insured her with Lloyds of London for an astronomical sum. The policy dictated that she would not be allowed to take up arms in warfare or join the army in peacetime. (It said nothing about military tap numbers.) It also stipulated (in a clause apparently written by W. C. Fields) that her insurance contract would not be valid if she met death by injury while intoxicated.

On the humorous side, rumors were started that Shirley was not really a child—she was a midget. And not just a midget—but a midget female impersonator! The Dies Committee of the U.S. House of Representatives (which investigated "un-American" activities in Hollywood during the thirties) labeled the nine-year-old Shirley a Communist dupe, an official "Red." Since the only red Shirley Temple knew anything about was the color in her own cheeks, the committee came off looking ludicrous.

Magazines reported these rumors and exaggerations. Stories said there was a fence around the Temple estate that would electrocute anyone who touched it. (Mrs. Temple was quick to point out that a fence like that would also electrocute Shirley, if her ball rolled against it in play.) Other reports said she was a billionaire, and some said all her money had been given to orphanages. One day the word was that she had a genius IQ, and the next day that she couldn't read or write. That she was dieting to get thin—and overeating to get fat. That she was in reality spoiled, and then that she was a perfect angel. Screenwriter Donald Ogden Stewart claimed that, when his son invited Shirley to a birthday party, word was sent that she could make a "personal appearance"—but only for a stipulated fat fee. There were alleged feuds between her and Jane Withers, and a rumor that she had snubbed Freddie Bartholomew when he asked to have his picture taken with her at the President's Ball.

But the stalwart Temples could take it all and survive. Each new

RLEY TEMPLE

nasty rumor, each new spiteful allegation, just seemed to strengthen them as a family and as a bastion of sanity. But one thing they could not—and did not—take in their stride was a review of *Wee Willie Winkie* by prominent British author Graham Greene.

Greene had reviewed several of Shirley's movies. When he first saw her on film, he had written of his expectation of the usual sentimental exploitation of childhood, but that, in seeing her, he had not "expected the tremendous energy which her rivals certainly lack." His review of *Captain January* referred to the film as "sentimental, a little depraved, with an appeal interestingly decadent." He did give Shirley her due, however, by saying that "Shirley Temple acts and dances with immense vigor and assurance, but some of her popularity seems to rest on a coquetry quite as mature as Miss Colbert's and on an oddly precocious body as voluptuous in grey flannel trousers as Miss Dietrich's."*

Finally, his review of *Wee Willie Winkie* became the subject of a celebrated libel case in which Shirley Temple and 20th Century-Fox sued Greene and his magazine (*Night and Day*) for libel. The statement of claim said Greene's review had accused the studio of

"procuring" Miss Temple "for immoral purposes." Shirley won her case and the action allegedly resulted in the collapse of the magazine, as London news distributors refused to sell the issue. More sober views of the situation indicate that *Night and Day* was already shaky and would have folded anyway. But it proved one thing —hell hath no fury like a baby badly reviewed!

Shirley Temple herself was not aware of the Greene libel case, nor was she aware of much of the publicity surrounding her. As far as she was concerned, her life was perfectly normal. She was up early in the morning, with a regimented breakfast of orange juice, cereal, coddled egg, and milk. Lunch was at noon, with vegetable or cream soup, a plate of two vegetables with chicken or lamb, and perhaps her favorite dessert of ice cream "with gravy" (or blanc mange or jello). Home at day's end to a dinner of vegetable, stewed fruit, and a big malted milk. No in-between snacks ever allowed and cod-liver oil twice a day. No variations in schedule. To bed early and lights turned out firmly.

By law, Shirley was permitted to be on a studio set for six hours a day, with three hours of actual camera work. Her mother was on the set at all times, having been put under contract by Fox (at a salary of $1,000

*Graham Greene, *Graham Greene on Film*, Simon and Schuster, New York, 1972, p.92.

96

With her parents at the circus, 1936

per week) to act as Shirley's "professional coach and governess." That way little Shirley could still spend the entire day in close contact with her sensible mother. She saw her father at breakfast and at night, when she had a story hour with him alone.

Mr. and Mrs. Temple tried to face the problems of raising their daughter in the limelight early on in her career. They decided to bank and invest Shirley's income, and live off their own combined salaries. They lived quietly at home, seldom going out, and stressing the life of a family with three children, not one child-star. Occasionally, they allowed themselves luxurious vacations, always with the children along, whenever Shirley had time off between movies. Mrs. Temple hired an all-around servant to cook meals and attend to the house while she was away at the studio. The mail was taken care of by two secretaries, one part-time and one full-time. The studio itself supplied a bodyguard for Shirley, who also drove Mrs. Temple and her daughter to work and back in their big LaSalle. There was no official chauffeur . . . and no butler, no maid.

Mrs. Temple was anxious to present what she considered a proper working atmosphere on the set. She insisted that no swearing be overheard by Shirley, or it was instant dismissal for the day. Shirley soon caught on to this, and remembers, "I'd hear Lionel Barrymore start in—he was in great pain, you know—and I'd think, Great! I'm going home early again today!" Despite these occasional slips, Mrs. Temple proudly told reporters, "It is an excellent experience in every way for Shirley. A clean, wholesome atmosphere surrounds her every minute, and she has never seen or heard a single thing that was detrimental. Mr. Temple and I both consider her contact with these charming, busy, ambitious people a splendid incentive."

Throughout Shirley's career as a superstar, Mrs. Temple remained something of a mystery, a tall, dark-haired woman who said little outside of official interviews and who then mostly talked about her daughter. Her father had died when she was fourteen, leaving her mother, younger brothers, and herself to fend as best they could. Mrs. Temple clearly knew how to take care of herself. Although she was willing to agree to such shenanigans as having the studio shave a year off Shirley's age—and to having Shirley pose for countless stills and advertising layouts—she was not willing to turn her head while her daughter's life was ruined.

And so she was there. Every day on the set, like the Rock of Gibraltar, sometimes standing by the camera and calling out, "Sparkle, Shirley, sparkle" during musical numbers. It was Mrs. Temple who answered reporters' questions and guided all interviews. It was Mrs. Temple who steered a firm course for the good ship Shirley Temple through the dangerous waters of public adulation and fan insanity. It was Mrs. Temple who was Shirley's official "boss." ("Shirley is my job, a twenty-four-hour-a-day job, for I am always with her.") Director Irving Cummings remarked on the set of *Poor Little Rich Girl*: "Mrs. Temple is much more Shirley's director than I am. She teaches her her lines, coaches her on how to say them, suggests Shirley's expressions, shows her how to sit and stand and talk and walk and run." Allan Dwan, who directed the child in three pictures, when asked what it was like to work with the young Temple, commented, "Well, to a degree, you worked through her mother, who had a great influence over her and used to work with her at home at night on the things she was to do the following day."

Mrs. Temple described her method of working with Shirley: "When she begins a new picture, I tell her the entire story in detail. It is sometimes uncanny how she grasps the adult problems. Then, at breakfast, I read the lines she is to speak in scenes that day and we go over each phrase, talking them naturally, just as if we were the people in the play. That is all she needs, for with her retentive memory she never forgets or transposes a word."

Interviewed by *Parents' Magazine* about the rigors of raising a child-star, Mrs. Temple explained her basic "spare the rod and spoil the star" formula. "We have been strict, very strict with her, and none of us spoil her. The responsibility for disciplining her is mine entirely, with no interference from her father or her brothers. When I speak, she minds. There is no argument, no pleading, no begging. I have never permitted any impudence, crying, or displays of temper. I have taught her to wait on herself and to be independent. And also, I have taught her not to be afraid of anything. . . . I began this training very early and it means constant vigilance. I soon learned not to let my affection make me too lenient—that is most harmful, for it brings trouble later on."

Pressed for her procedures on discipline, Mrs. Temple claimed, "I've never punished her in my life. I just don't have to." Later she added more candidly, "My most effective punishment at present is removing her plate at dinner while she is sent to her room until peace is restored. Oh, yes, Shirley has had a few paddlings. When a child is very young you have to be direct in corrections."

Mrs. Temple was in a sense the Dr. Spock of her day, as everyone wanted to know what the magic formula was. Magazines couldn't get enough of Mrs. Temple's advice to mothers, and one story even detailed how Shirley had been fed by what was demurely referred to as "nature's method" the first four months. Occasionally, Mrs. Temple could be persuaded to talk about her own feelings about her daughter. "Shirley is my dream-daughter come true. I always wanted a little girl, but when two fine sons came it seemed as if our family was complete. My life became filled with domestic and social duties and I had almost given up the idea of another baby. But the desire for a daughter persisted, and I knew I'd never be contented until she came. I wanted her to be artistic. I was determined she should *excel* at something."

Excel she did. And Mrs. Temple

Shirley and Mrs. Temple

never had any regrets or showed any indication that she felt her daughter's career had been anything but a wonderful experience. Throughout all the madness, Mrs. Temple always knew she had that one contractual clause (the cancellation right) as a straw in the wind to clutch at: "The mother of a famous child-star has a difficult road to travel. If the day ever comes when I feel that Shirley is becoming self-conscious or too aware of her screen importance, I shall cancel her contract immediately."

There was an old Hollywood formula: mix together one talented child, one movie set, and one stage mother—and you've got trouble. Gertrude Temple and her daughter, Shirley Jane, were that inevitable exception that proved the rule.

I can't wait till I grow up. I don't know exactly why I want to so much. I think, perhaps, I have had enough of childhood. I think you have even more fun when you grow up. I don't know what, but there is more . . . isn't there?"

Shirley Temple, interviewed on the set of *Miss Annie Rooney*, 1942.

JUNIOR MRS.

The rumblings began when the financial returns first started coming in on *The Blue Bird*. When *Young People* also fared poorly at the box office, the rumblings became a discontented roar. Without a moment's hesitation, Mrs. Temple announced her daughter's retirement from films with all the solemnity and drama of a royal abdication, which in a way is exactly what it was. Exercising her option to cancel, Mrs. Temple bought out the rest of Shirley's Fox contract (which had some time to go) in 1940, reportedly at a cost to the Temples of $300,000.

Publicly, Mrs. Temple stated that it was time for her daughter to go to school with other girls and get through her awkward period without the eyes of the world trained upon her. Privately, she blamed Shirley's box-office slump on bad scripts. Publicly, Fox executives discussed the loss of the foreign market to the war and the impending talk of United States involvement. Privately, they merely pointed their fingers at the red ink

under Shirley's name on their books, and that was that. Shirley Temple, the sweetheart of the thirties, was a has-been at age twelve. Gone were the days when Bill Robinson called her "Butch" and Gary Cooper dubbed her "Wiggle Britches." Now it was out the door, thank you, ma'am, with a few old costumes and her little white rehearsal piano to remember it all by.

Within a short time, however, it was announced that Shirley had signed a new contract with Metro-Goldwyn-Mayer—forty weeks at $2,500 per week. Louis B. Mayer's famous love of child-stars was too great for him to resist the opportunity of signing the one he had always wanted to have—Little Miss Marker. (However, Mr. Mayer did *not* sign Mrs. Temple to a contract as "coach"—that was the sort of job he liked to reserve for himself.)

Never having recovered from the shock of losing Deanna Durbin to Universal, Mayer hoped to bring out a film to co-star Durbin and Temple, to be produced by Joe Pasternak, Durbin's mentor. But Universal refused to lend Durbin, and when Shirley somehow seemed inappropriate for the down-to-earth show-business background of a proposed role in a Rooney-Garland

KATHLEEN (1941). With Gail Patrick, Herbert Marshall, and Laraine Day

film, both projects were scrapped. Instead, Shirley's first (and only) film at MGM was a teen-age soap opera.

Released late in 1941, *Kathleen* is a chip off the old Temple marzipan. Once again she is the poor little rich girl with a mean governess and a neglectful father. This time she's old enough (twelve years) to sneak out and find her own father-substitute in character actor Felix Bressart. Otherwise, it's just the same old march toward her daddy's lap, although Metro-Goldwyn-Mayer did not miss the opportunity to present one of its famous House and Gardens homes, complete with servants, sterling silver, and grandiose living room.

When Kathleen (Shirley Temple) rigs up a harmless amateur bomb to surprise her governess' snooping, her father calls in a psychiatrist. This good doctor advises the father to engage a beautiful child psychologist (Laraine Day) as his daughter's companion. Romance blossoms between daddy (Herbert Marshall) and doctor (Day), although not without a few plot twists involving a gold-digging Gail Patrick and a runaway Shirley.

At this age, Shirley Temple is a pretty little girl, not at all an awkward adolescent, but not yet the lovely young woman she became. She wears her first long dress on screen, and is subjected to a few "glamour close-ups," the signature of her new home studio. (Also in the great MGM tradition, the script does not miss a chance to promote other studio stars. When Gail Patrick suggests Shirley may have a crush on someone, she offers the names of Robert Taylor and Clark Gable.)

Kathleen's fantasies of love and romance include one ridiculous episode in which she imagines herself becoming a famous stage star. Done in lavish MGM style (albeit without Technicolor), the musical number in this scene is more nightmare than dream. An army of phony soldiers in fancy dress uniform is singing away insanely at the bottom of an elegant staircase, and at the top is Shirley Temple, ludicrously gowned in ostrich feathers and white tulle. Even more ludicrous, out of her mouth comes a soprano voice, obviously dubbed, trilling away in mock Durbin style. Temple later sings in a simpler, smaller voice (also apparently dubbed) and tries to dance with the soldiers, who lift and carry her as if she has a broken leg.

The audience is confronted with one suddenly apparent horror: as an adult, Shirley Temple could neither sing nor dance! Or at least she could not sing and dance well enough to make the grade in a studio which boasted Kelly, Astaire, Garland, Powell, and Miller—and which became the most innovative studio in the musical genre during the decade which was just beginning.

In the past, Temple's films had

KATHLEEN (1941). With Felix Bressart

MISS ANNIE ROONEY (1942). With Dickie Moore and friends

more or less been small, like her, or at least intimate. Her musical numbers had been charming interludes, deliberately amateurish as befitted her young years. At MGM, the sets and the production required professionals of enormous talent to impress their personalities on the often over-mounted productions. Temple just couldn't handle it. In an MGM musical, she was as out-of-place as Lassie would have been in *Private Lives.* When *Kathleen* was released to indifferent reviews, the MGM contract was canceled by mutual consent of both parties.

Shirley's last film before her official "comeback" under the David O. Selznick banner was *Miss Annie Rooney,* an Edward Small Produc-

tion released through United Artists. It is a sorry finish to her childhood career. Based on an original screenplay by George Bruce, *Miss Annie Rooney* is a budget production which uses Shirley's already established screen *persona* to pad out a flimsy story. The old star quality is gone—even the once golden curls are now dark and brushed down smoothly. Shirley does her best with forties "jive" dialogue that has her throwing around lines such as "Hi-ya superman," "How divinely snakey," and "he's a dater from Decatur." Nothing helps to cover the threadbare plot about a father (William Gargan), who chases get-rich-quick schemes, and a "wrong side of the tracks" love story between Shirley and a rich boy friend (Dickie Moore), from whom she gets her first screen "kiss"—a much-publicized peck that is as insubstantial as the plot. (When asked what it felt like, Shirley told interviewers, "Like a butterfly—it tickled.")

Suddenly, Shirley Temple, once a top money-maker and princess of the Fox lot, was picking her way through a haphazard cheapie which seemed to have been ripped off from an old Joan Crawford movie. This was no way to end a wildly successful career—and Mrs. Temple called a halt.

After *Miss Annie Rooney*, Shirley Temple did not make a film for two years. During that time she lived the life of a typical American teenager. Or, if not the life of a typical American teenager, at least as close to that ideal as any millionaire ex-child-star could get. Shortly after her "retirement" from 20th Century-Fox, her mother had enrolled her in the exclusive school for girls, Miss Westlake's, and she continued her education there. She was popular with her classmates, graduating with a respectable but relatively undistinguished academic career (an overall B average indicating her genius IQ might have been a press agent's dream).

After her graduation, her "comeback" was announced, and she signed a personal contract with David O. Selznick, who also had under contract such stars as Ingrid Bergman, Jennifer Jones, Joseph Cotten, and Robert Walker. For her official return to films, Selznick selected his most prestigious effort since his epic-making *Gone With the Wind*—a sentimental tribute to the American family during World War II, to be called *Since You Went Away*.

The opening legend gives the film's raison d'être: "This is the story of an Unconquerable Fortress . . . The American Home, 1943." Selznick himself worked on the screenplay ("screenplay by the producer", reads his modest credit), which concerns the adjustment of a family to the changes war brings to their lives—most notably the enlistment of the family's father, who is never seen on screen.

Shirley Temple is billed fourth, after Claudette Colbert, Jennifer Jones, and Joseph Cotten, and her screen time is relatively limited, considering the overall running time of the film which, like *Gone With the Wind*, originally contained an intermission. Despite her small role, and some of the film's maudlin content, Temple's return to movies can only be considered a success. In fact, most of the initial audience interest was in her. In one of his celebrated memos, Selznick wrote, "I'm anxious to get the accent off this as a Temple vehicle and start hammering away at its tremendous cast."

The accent of the final film was indeed off the idea of a "Temple vehicle." The film was meant to present the American home front in a series of episodes, with the main theme being "civilian sacrifices." Since these sacrifices ranged all the way from the mother having to give up her maid to the combat death of the older daughter's sweetheart, a lot of ground was covered. Shirley Temple plays Brig, the younger daughter of the house, and makes an ideal example of that relic of World War II, the all-American girl. With her ruffled pockets, her locket on a chain, and her hair ribbons, she looks, acts, and talks like the typical wartime teenager.

And why not? In her two years off screen, Shirley had become a typical teenager. "Brig was a breeze," she told an interviewer. "I knew all about her right from the beginning because she was practically me." Furthermore, she was on familiar territory as the dimpled darling of the household who speaks her mind frankly and stands for no nonsense. Her handling of Monty Woolley, that seasoned alumnus of the crusty-old-codger school of acting, was easier than selling war bonds at a Gold Star Mother's rally. After all, she'd had much more experience in the game than he had.

Most of the movie-going public identified strongly with *Since You Went Away*. It was about the world they lived in and understood, and it praised them for their part in the war effort. As an example of forties nostalgia, it is a first-rate piece of cinema, ably directed by John Cromwell. The viewer is transported into a world in which young girls with flowers in their hair dance with soldiers in an airplane hangar. (When the band swings into "The Dipsy Doodle," one feels inspired to go out and plant a victory garden.) It is a world in which service stars are hanging in the windows, and "Loose Lips Sink Ships" signs are posted on every wall. People are counting ration points and pouring milk out of glass bottles instead of paper cartons. A neon sign alternately flashes "Paradise Cocktail Lounge"—and then—"Buy War Bonds."

Shirley's role in *Since You Went Away* is not really central to the film's action. Yet, as she collects salvage and buys war stamps at school, she seems utterly believable and completely sincere. And even if the public felt a bit unnerved to see the tyke suddenly wearing high heels and lipstick, it was still an auspicious return to the screen.

Her next film, *I'll Be Seeing You*, made for Selznick in 1945, is a low-budget companion piece to *Since You Went Away*. Again, the film was about the American home front during World War II, a world

SINCE YOU WENT AWAY (1944). With Joseph Cotten, Jennifer Jones, and Claudette Colbert

of no gum and no chocolate bars, but apparently no shortage of syrup, at least in the screenwriting department.

Ginger Rogers plays a prisoner on parole for the Christmas holidays, and Joseph Cotten is a shell-shocked war hero released from a sanitarium on a trial run. (A voice-over tells us about the problems of "the neuropsychiatric soldier.") Rogers and Cotten meet and fall in love, and Shirley Temple again has a peripheral role as Rogers' niece. In this, she has even less footage than in *Since You Went Away*, but looks even more grown up. As she enters the film for the first time, Temple is greeted by Rogers with the words, "Hello, Barbara. Why, I never would have known you. You've grown into a beauty," probably echoing what the entire American audience was thinking at that moment.

Shirley is petite and perky, and plays with a relaxed manner which has not entirely lost the sense of fun and mischief she had as a child. Much of the strength of the film lies in the family scenes of which she is an integral part: the simple Christmas Eve around the dinner table, the very forties New Year's Dance. A small picture, done with good taste despite its sentimental script, *I'll Be Seeing You* was designed for a wartime audience who would accept its messages.

At the age of sixteen, Shirley

SINCE YOU WENT AWAY (1944). With Claudette Colbert

granted her very first "grown-up" interview to Louella Parsons, a Hollywood rite of passage. Louella pointed out that it was indeed a "grown-up" interview, the first Shirley had ever given without her mother present. As Louella told it, " . . . the first time she has ever talked with the press without benefit of Mama Temple, who, in past endeavors was not only present —but usually put the words in Shirley's mouth and the ideas in her curly head." Although the article went on to admit grudging respect for Mrs. Temple, it was clear that interviewers were now anxious to find out what the older Shirley had

to say on her own—if anything.

Shirley, however, still liked her mother to be with her on the set. (One interviewer entitled her article, "Life with Mother.") In general, Mrs. Temple was still on the job, watching over Shirley's development, laying down strict rules about who she could date and what time she had to come home. But Shirley was beginning to do a few things for herself—choosing her own clothes for the first time and wearing as much powder and paint as she could get away with. Her former playhouse now rocked with the music of teen-age dances and rang with the shouts of friends who came to swim at the Temple estate.

Although Gertrude Temple had done her best not to be a stage-mama, she had nevertheless devoted her life to carefully managing her daughter's affairs. Many felt this management continued too long after Shirley had reached her young adulthood. Although Shirley clearly loved her mother, friends guessed the time would soon come when she would need to break out to find herself. A girl who worked closely with Shirley prophesied, "She'll marry early, you'll see—to get away from her mother."

In the meantime, Shirley liked to describe herself as a "chic chick" who subscribed to the Book-of-the-Month Club and who liked noisy radio serials. As to her career, she had a new slant on it: "Acting is different these days. Then I could just kind of gurgle and get what I wanted. Gurgling just isn't the answer anymore. Not with Mr. Selznick anyway."

Shirley's next movie, produced by Sol Seigel for Columbia, was based on F. Hugh Herbert's long-running Broadway success, *Kiss and Tell*. It is a thoroughly unlikable picture. It has almost no real laughs in it, and what few there are have unpleasant overtones. The characters of the Archer family were

I'LL BE SEEING YOU (1944). With Spring Byington

I'LL BE SEEING YOU (1944). As Barbara Marshall

part of the forties scene (much like Henry Aldrich or Archie and his friends). Made widely popular by a radio show, "Meet Corliss Archer" (which went on the air soon after the film's release), the family consisted of Corliss (Shirley Temple), her parents (Walter Abel and Katharine Alexander), and her older brother, Lenny (Scott Elliott). Other characters of the situation comedy were Corliss' boy friend, Dexter (Jerome Courtland), who shouted "Holy Cow!" at any provocation, and her best friend, Mildred (Virginia Welles).

In *Kiss and Tell* Mildred secretly marries Lenny and becomes pregnant. Since the two families are feuding and Lenny is off to war, Corliss accompanies Mildred to the doctor and is herself suspected of the pregnancy. Cruel jokes based on ugly innuendoes form the basis of this comedy of manners, and the portrait of an American family who care more about their reputation than about their daughter's well-being is downright venal. (The amount of shouting, yelling, dog-kicking, and neighbor-punching done by Mr. Archer is enough to offset forever those kindly, understanding fathers who appeared on television in the fifties.)

Shirley Temple is really too sweet for the character of Corliss Archer. She lacks the low-down vamp instinct that was written into the orig-inal character, a conniving teen-age femme fatale who twisted all males around her finger. Although *Time* called her "a first-rate comedienne" in its review, her playing is too bland to be really effective. *Kiss and Tell* is best summed up by the oft-repeated tag line of Mildred's younger brother (Darryl Hickman): "I think it's all very dumb."

During the filming of *Kiss and Tell*, a world-sobering event took place: Shirley Jane Temple announced her engagement to John George Agar—and everybody said, "My, how the years have flown" . . . "Can it be possible?" . . . "Oh, how she's grown" and all the things adults feel obliged to say when confronted with the fact that someone they thought was a baby had suddenly grown up behind their backs.

Shirley Temple had met John Agar sometime during 1943 when she was only fifteen. They had originally met through Agar's sister, Joyce, who had been introduced to Shirley by ZaSu Pitts' daughter, Ann Gallary. Ann, like Shirley, was a student at Westlake, and the two families were neighbors. At the time of the engagement, Shirley had known Agar for nearly two years.

John George Agar (whose first names, as Shirley never got tired of pointing out, were her brothers' names, too) was seven years older than his fiancée. He was a

KISS AND TELL (1945). With Virginia Welles

physical-training instructor at nearby March Field, and he was tall and handsome in his uniform. He had been vaguely engaged in "laboratory work" before he went into the service, and it was said that he might "return to the firm his father started," the Agar Packing Company in Chicago.

Not much else was known about Agar—and not much else seemed to matter, except that he was engaged to America's Very Own Little Girl. When the engagement was originally announced, the young couple promised to wait two years. But the world was at war. Shirley's brothers were away in the armed forces

(George had been at Pearl Harbor during the attack), and Agar was an enlisted man. Shirley convinced her parents that these were not years in which young couples could—or should—wait.

And so, on the evening of September 19, 1945, at 8:30 P.M., the world felt a little older as Miss Shirley wed Sergeant John. When the appointed hour approached, over 15,000 fans assembled outside the church and climbed on lamp posts for a better view. They invaded the pastor's study and clattered over the roof of the church. They screamed and yelled and some of them fainted. Inside, seven bridesmaids and one maid of honor came down the aisle of the Wilshire Methodist Church wearing a shade that was later officially named Temple blue—followed by Shirley herself in lustrous white satin, heavily studded with seed pearls. Carrying a bouquet of white orchids and trailing a white tulle veil which flowed from an appropriate "little princess" crown, Shirley Temple became a bride as the sounds of the fans' feet clumped overhead on the church rooftop. Their screams, shrieks, and shenanigans were in the great tradition of celebrity weddings.

A reception for five hundred invited guests followed at the Temple family estate. The arbor was festooned with garlands of roses, and pairs of porcelain turtledoves were perched on the ridgepoles. The gifts on display included a complete set of silverware with service for twelve (chosen from stock available under wartime restrictions), all engraved with the initial A, a sterling tea service, a crystal service for twelve, Spode chinaware, a 22-carat gold berry set, presumably for solid gold berries, and much more. It was like the riches that were displayed in

With John Agar, after the birth of their baby

19

her old films to tempt Depression appetites.

With suitable fanfare, Shirley Temple had become a Junior Mrs. The roses bloomed, and the champagne flowed. The moon came out and bathed the two-and-a-half hour receiving line in white light. The band played, and everyone smiled. Of her bridegroom, whose entire family reportedly planned to move at once to California, Shirley officially said, "He's the handsomest, most intelligent, most charming, adorable boy ever born." It was all Lohengrin and happiness . . . at least that evening, under the moonlight, in the shadow of the playhouse.

The announcement of the address for the new Sergeant and Mrs. John G. Agar was prophetic; home was to be her old playhouse, strategically situated on the Temple family estate. This was the famous house with the stage, trap-drum set, soda fountain, and doll collection. It also included a projection room and two downstairs rooms which held all of the souvenirs and milestones of Shirley's fabulous career, including costumes from all her pictures. Symbolically, the big stage was torn out to make way for a bedroom.

Off on a secret honeymoon, under the names of Emil and Emma Glutz, the young Agars had stars in their eyes. Shirley left behind her Ten Rules for a Happy Honeymoon for the fan magazines to publish. ("Be careful not to attract any male attention except your groom's and don't let your own happiness make you selfish or thoughtless.") The ghost of Gertrude Temple's stoic code of conduct echoed in the child-like list of rules.

When the Agars settled down to life together, the news media went berserk. The American public became as eager now to hear about their "big girl" (as one story was titled) as they had been when she was still small. One fan magazine article gushed, "Golly! What fun for Shirley, who thinks being mistress of the pots and pans is simply

AFTER THE HAPPILY EVER AFTER

super." When asked about her husband's after-service plans, Shirley seemed vague: "He studied business administration in school, so I guess it will be business of some kind. But I don't know what field . . ."

While Agar finished his enlistment, Shirley was announced for a Selznick project, *Little Women*, to co-star her with Jennifer Jones, Dorothy McGuire, and Diana Lynn. Filming was abandoned after three months, however, and Shirley (along with Guy Madison, another *Little Women* derelict) was sent over to RKO to make a film entitled *Honeymoon*. (Since her own honeymoon was such a recent event, no doubt the shrewd businessmen at RKO felt this was a good title for box-office potential.)

Honeymoon capitalized on the idea of Temple as a young bride, as it told an involved story about a young girl from Minnesota who comes to Mexico to wed her soldier sweetheart. Facing untold legal complications, they engage the help of an American vice-consul, played by Franchot Tone. During the thirties, it might have been done with style, wit, a cast of funny supporting characters, and a maximum of laughter. As a 1947 release, it suf-

HONEYMOON (1947). With Guy Madison

fered from tired blood, and with its mockery of young marriage and love, it seemed to be making indirect fun of its leading lady. Both Franchot Tone and Shirley did their professional best to take it seriously. As the young soldier, Guy Madison was super-handsome in the clean-cut, Robert Redford style, but his acting was too dull to make him a star. The public received *Honeymoon* with little enthusiasm.

But the next film for Shirley was a winner on all counts. Based on an original story and screenplay by Sidney Sheldon, *The Bachelor and the Bobby-Soxer* boasted not only Shirley in the cast (the title card read "Miss Temple's services by arrangement with David O. Selznick"), but also two masters of the deft comic touch, Cary Grant and Myrna Loy. Loy and Temple play sisters, and any potential embarrassment over this odd situation is dealt with directly: "Is this your daughter?" asks a catty rival for Grant's attention to Loy.

A bright script finds Loy (a judge) forcing Grant to pretend to be Temple's boy friend, or he will be sentenced to a long jail term. Grant's hilarious antics in adjusting to the slang and mannerisms of an adolescent generation make a wonderfully funny situation. Shirley has by now fulfilled the physical promise of her childhood—she is an extremely pretty young lady, with a creamy complexion, thick, curly hair, and sparkling eyes. Her playing of a typical teenager is the opposite of her roles in *Since You Went Away* and *I'll Be Seeing You*. In those two serious films, she provided a low-key, honest portrait of the all-American girl. Here she is the comic counterpart of those two young women: satirically mocking the self-importance and exaggerated behavior of those years. Her performance indicates that, with good material, she might have become a competent comedienne. Her husky speaking voice is particularly pleasant, and her delivery of lines shows the understanding and good timing she was famous for as a child.

In *The Bachelor and the Bobby-Soxer*, she was working with the sort of supporting cast that could have swamped her, but she more than holds her own. For once, critics wrote enthusiastically about a Temple adult film: "Shirley Temple is such an attractive young actress," wrote *Commonweal*. "She is a sweet young girl, the audiences are enchanted with her, and that's that," said *The New Republic*. It is a credit to Grant and Temple's deft handling of their roles that at no time does the idea of a man Grant's age pretending involvement with a girl Shirley's age seem distasteful. (On the contrary, one can't help but feel intrigued about the idea of her dim-

THE BACHELOR AND THE BOBBY-SOXER (1947). With Cary Grant

ples mating with the cleft in his chin! Would the child look like Kirk Douglas?) Cary Grant's "hoo-doo" routine in the film passed into the folklore of the late forties, and Shirley had herself a hit.

Following the release of *The Bachelor and the Bobby-Soxer*, rumors of trouble in the Agar marriage became frequent. Much to her shock, Shirley found out that Agar had once had an unsuccessful career as a professional singer with a Chicago band. Even more shocking, he had been given a Hollywood screen test before his enlistment, which he had failed. He now announced his desire for a screen career, something which was totally unexpected by Shirley and her family. (As it turned out, the Agar "business in Chicago" had been sold in 1935.)

Shirley now went into a film which she later referred to as her best adult movie, *That Hagen Girl*. ("I'm not too proud of the movies I made as a grown-up except *That Hagen Girl*, which nobody remembers but which gave me a chance to act.")

That Hagen Girl did give Shirley a chance to act. What she did with it is another story. (Bosley Crowther wrote in the *Times:* "She acts with the mopish dejection of a school-child who has just been robbed of a two-scoop ice cream cone.") In this turgid drama about American small-town life, she plays an adopted child (always the orphan!) whose life is plagued by gossip and rumor about illegitimacy. Shirley is called upon to do a scene from *Romeo and Juliet* (it comes out more like *Hansel and Gretel*) and even throws herself in the lagoon before the situation is straightened out. Her romantic lead in this film, oddly enough, is that other stalwart conservative Republican from the state of California, Ronald Reagan. Even odder is their relationship: after being suspected of being her father for the entire film, Reagan suddenly sweeps the teenager into his arms at the finish. Shirley Temple—the little girl who sang to her father about "marry me and let me be your wife"—almost made her goal in a grown-up film!

Following his discharge from the service, John Agar was put under contract by David O. Selznick. In order to capitalize on the publicity value of their marriage, they were co-starred in Shirley's next film, *Fort Apache*, the one really distinguished movie she made as an adult. Directed by John Ford, who had guided her through *Wee Willie Winkie* eleven years earlier, it can hardly be called a Shirley Temple film even by the wildest stretch of the imagination. However, her character ("Philadelphia") shows much of the spunk and candor of the little girls Shirley played as a child. Unfortunately, Shirley plays the role as if she were still Wee Willie Winkie, and although her performance does not mar this beautiful

THE BACHELOR AND THE BOBBY-SOXER (1947). With Myrna Loy

THAT HAGEN GIRL (1947). With Ronald Reagan

example of the Western film, it does nothing in particular to enhance it either.

Shirley's love interest in the film is played by her husband, who was no great actor. Public interest in the young couple was high, however, and their presence together as the romantic leads boosted the box-office appeal of the film. The film's real strength and meaning lies in the relationship of the two leads, Henry Fonda and John Wayne, and in the poetry and sadness that characterize the work of John Ford.

After *Fort Apache*, the Agars' daughter and only child was born. In announcing the impending birth, Shirley made an ominous statement: "If there is any one thing I wish for my baby it is this: That she grow up to be independent, standing on her own feet, leading her own life."

On January 30, 1948, their daughter was born and named

Linda Susan. It was a story which made headlines around the world, ("The Baby Has a Baby"), and the major question that was on everyone's mind was . . . does she look like the little Shirley Temple or not?

"It's the lullabye story of the year," gushed Louella Parsons, who reported that the young mother craved chocolate cookies with white icing. She went on to assure her readers that this baby had the exact same dimple in the cheek in the exact same spot as her famous mother. And to verify this information came the official word: the dimple had been discovered by none other than Gertrude Temple herself.

By now the rumors about the Agar marriage (and Shirley's continued dependence on her mother) were more than rumors—they were "out in the open" Hollywood facts. Shirley issued a statement, "When I was expecting my baby—and still able to be in a picture—Mother went with me to the studio. She felt there were so many physical things she could help me with and spare me." Agar said little, joshingly admitting that they sometimes quarreled, but . . . as Louella herself told it in classic Hollywood jargon, "These two kids, instead of skirting problems that have wrecked some Hollywood marriages, bring them out in the open . . . and then forget them."

Perhaps hoping to squelch the rumors, and perhaps hoping pri-

FORT APACHE (1948). With Jack Pennick, Victor McLaglen, and John Agar

With John Agar and daughter Linda

vately that working together could help them, the Agars announced their intentions to star together in a film for RKO, a Dore Schary production to be called *Adventure in Baltimore*. (One wag described the title as a contradiction in terms.) Based on an original story by Lesser Samuels and Christopher Isherwood, it is a minor film in every way, but Shirley Temple has a good role as a young woman who today would be called a "women's libber." Since the film is a period piece, she is known as a suffragette, although she is too addle-headed to be classed as anyone that strongly motivated. *Adventure in Baltimore* is a family situation-comedy, and even stars that stalwart television "father"—Robert Young, cast here as an Episcopalian minister who is Shirley's sympathetic papa. Since Shirley's rebellion consists mainly of wanting to be a painter (and of daring to wear only two petticoats instead of the standard five), his sympathy isn't all that impressive. Shirley lacks any real fire in a role which requires the sort of zip she had as a child-star. Nevertheless, *Adventure in Baltimore* (retitled *Baltimore Escapade* for television release) has a certain low-key charm. The flimsy material lacks zest and sparkle, but its gentle quality is unmistakably honest and in the tradition of the Americana film genre.

Adventure in Baltimore has one beautiful scene: when Shirley is scorned by her peers at a dance —and the romantic lead (Agar) snubs her to dance with a flirtatious belle—her father takes her onto the floor for the waltz contest. Since his secret is that he once toured vaudeville as a dancer, he is able to give his forlorn daughter one small moment of sweet triumph. They win the contest in a twirling, swirling, and lyrically executed dance, with Shirley's white dress flying around her. As she realizes what is happening, Shirley throws back her head, and flashing the dimpled smile, now gloriously mature and womanly, she cries out: "Oh, papa—we've won!" *Adventure in Baltimore* may be lackluster in the main, but for one brief moment it gives audiences the Shirley Temple they had expected to grow out of that vital and talented child they used to know.

Shirley continued to work. She next returned to the studio that had "kissed her off" in 1940: it was over to 20th Century-Fox to co-star in *Mr. Belvedere Goes to College*, a sequel to the enormously popular *Sitting Pretty* (1948). Fox paid Selznick a whopping $100,000 to use Shirley . . . and then let the opportunity go totally to waste.

Sitting Pretty, one of Fox's big hits of the postwar period, had introduced movie-going audiences to the character of "Lynn Belvedere."

ADVENTURE IN BALTIMORE (1949). With Robert Young and Josephine Hutchinson

Belvedere was a superior man—one who wrote best-selling novels, cooked, gardened, sang and danced, worked complicated math problems in his head—and who even baby-sat with the utmost elegance and capability. Audiences found his particular brand of snobbery hilarious—and they identified with his ability to deflate pomposity. Belvedere—played right up to the eyebrows by Clifton Webb—gave audiences a vicarious thrill by always coming out on top in every situation through his triumphant intelligence and brilliant maneuvering.

Sitting Pretty proved so successful that Fox decided on a sequel. (A third film, *Mr. Belvedere Rings the Bell*, was also made.) In this far from riotous movie, Belvedere is forced to return to college as an undergraduate, a degree being required for his collecting a $10,000 cash prize from a literary award. (So far, Belvedere's formal schooling has consisted of "two revolting weeks in kindergarten.") On the campus, Belvedere meets Shirley, a war widow with a young son, who for mysterious reasons is trying to keep her marriage a secret. Shirley merely plays stooge to Webb's outrageous camping. All the laughs are his, and one can't help but yearn for the days when a crusty old windbag like Belvedere would have found himself holding Shirley on his knee—while she not only stole his heart, but his show, too.

The Shirley Temple of *Mr. Belvedere Goes to College* is pretty, fresh-faced, and wholesome. Her adult voice is soft and slightly husky, with a pleasant quality. But not only does her acting seem totally inadequate for the situation —she is just plain boring on film, seemingly disinterested in most of the proceedings.

Following the Belvedere episode, Shirley Temple's adult film career wound down to an embarrassing finish. She made two more films: *The Story of Seabiscuit* for Warner Brothers and *A Kiss for Corliss* for Strand Productions, released by United Artists.

The Story of Seabiscuit, directed by David Butler, her old friend from Fox, proved to be her poorest adult movie, for which she received her worst personal reviews. Her characterization of an Irish colleen, complete with a labored brogue which seems to slip a little toward West Los Angeles from time to time, brought derisive comments from critics. The film itself fared little better, although Barry Fitzgerald performed well as Shirley's uncle, the Irish trainer of the great racehorse, Seabiscuit. (Lon McCallister, that young man who played second fiddle to so many animals in

MR. BELVEDERE GOES TO COLLEGE (1949). With Tom Drake and Clifton Webb

THE STORY OF SEABISCUIT (1949).
With Barry Fitzgerald

his short career, is once again seen leading a horse around and feebly providing romantic interest.) The film displays some strength, however, in the authentic racing scenes, especially the big race with Seabiscuit against War Admiral at Pimlico. The inclusion of actual newsreel footage strikes a note of much-needed reality. The horse steals the show, and is described as "small in body but big in heart." It is a sign of the passing of the times that, in the old days, that heart-warming tribute would have gone to the film's leading lady!

Finally, Shirley made her last film. When Marcus Loew, Richard Wallace, and Colin Miller formed their Strand Productions company, they fashioned another film based on the Corliss Archer character and hired Shirley to star. A Kiss for Corliss, later called Almost a Bride on television, was another distasteful story about a teenager, this time rumored to be having an affair with a much-married older man (David Niven). The original script had to be rewritten several times, as the Motion Picture Production Association was unhappy with its apparent light treatment of divorce. But rewritten or not, it was still a disaster—the last feature film ever made by Shirley Temple. Her own not-so-light treatment of the subject of divorce was in the offing.

Aware of the knocking she had taken at the hands of critics for her adult films, Shirley remarked, "Some of the critics say I've done a poor job. Maybe I have. But I defy anyone to have done a better job with the vapid, spineless characters I've been handed. I don't intend to play any more of them. If a good part comes along, fine. If it never comes along, that'll be fine, too." With this strong and definite statement, Shirley Temple not only showed her indifference to her adult career, but something else, too: she now was beginning to stand on her own two feet, and finally, to grow up.

There was other evidence of this "growing up." Shirley Temple, raised to put her best foot forward on all occasions, had long been unhappy in her marriage but had hidden it from her public. When it came to putting a good face on things, she knew what to do: she ate the spinach. For four years she had been trying to make a go of it, but now it had finally become too much. After a split-up and a reconciliation, she finally gave up and filed for a divorce against Agar, charging grievous mental cruelty. She asked custody of Linda Susan, and the right to resume her maiden name.

Insiders said that when Shirley married, she was still looking for someone to manage her. Agar had been more interested in the parties

A KISS FOR CORLISS (1949). With Darryl Hickman

and the dancing, of Hollywood celebrity life—not to mention a career of his own. Shirley tried to apologize for him: "It isn't easy for Jack. He is ambitious. He will never be happy as 'Mr. Temple.' " Agar had taken on a formidable assignment when he became the first husband of the little girl all Americans felt responsible for. It was, in all fairness to him, simply more than he could handle. It was reported that, at the wedding ceremony, Agar had been reminded by a guest, "Young man, remember, you are marrying an American *institution*." Agar had replied, "Yes, sir, and I promise to take good care of it—I mean, her."

In announcing her decision to divorce, Shirley had carried out the last of her dutiful acts as a Hollywood commodity: she had telephoned Louella Parsons to give her the news. According to that stalwart queen of gossip, Shirley had said, "I want our separation and divorce to be dignified. John is a nice boy, but he's a little mixed up."

To Sheilah Graham, second-string gossip queen, she added, "The trouble with my marriage started two and a half years ago when Jack started to drink . . . it has become unbearable."

Agar, who had been arrested on drunk-driving charges in 1950 and 1951, went home to mother and announced he would not contest Shirley's action. "I agree with Shirley that it must be done in a dignified manner." Unfortunately for the Agars, "dignified" Hollywood divorces were as much a part of storybook unreality as the romances that brought them on in the first place. There were the inevitable false and painful rumors. Johnnie Johnston and his wife, Kathryn Grayson (who later divorced), accused golfer Joe Kirkwood, Jr. (who played comic-strip boxer Joe Palooka on screen) of trying to promote a romance between Johnston and Shirley. (What Kirkwood's motives were remained unclear!) This was more a publicity stunt for the three principals involved than any truth about Shirley Temple, but the rumors were reprinted in national magazines and caused the Temple family great pain.

Shirley's testimony at the divorce trial shocked everyone. She told of Agar's neglect of her, his fondness for drinking, and his equally shocking fondness for other women. To a stunned public, the word was also out—Shirley had even contemplated suicide at one point. ("After dinner, I jumped in my car. I was going to drive over a cliff or something, but instead I drove to the doctor.")

Finally and utterly, the legion of Temple fans could no longer ignore the fact that little Shirley had truly grown up, as she completed the final ritual of the Hollywood-coming-of-age: her very own messy divorce.

If I marry again, I'll definitely stop pictures for good; the main reason being that you couldn't get me to marry an actor or anyone connected with motion pictures. I know I could never be happy, torn between the private and professional things. I know now the kind of person I am. Normal home life appeals to me, the same as normal school life used to. Must be nice, to go your own way and attend to your own affairs, with no rumors or questions or flash bulbs mixing in.

Shirley Temple, 1950.

On December 5, 1950, Shirley Temple's divorce from John Agar became final. In a sense, her decree was her graduation diploma from everything it had meant to be Shirley Temple. She had completed the traditional Hollywood cycle: bit player, overnight success, fabulous star, washed-up has-been, actress on the "comeback" trail, heartbroken divorcee. Now she was free to start a new and different kind of life.

On December 16th, less than two weeks later, she did exactly that by marrying Charles Alden Black, a San Francisco businessman she had met while on vacation in Hawaii, trying to forget the divorce.

Black, who was ten years older than Shirley, was everything she had thought Agar was: a solid citizen (he had gone to Harvard Business School), a war hero (Silver Star),

MRS. CHARLES BLACK, CITIZEN

and the son of a prominent California businessman (his father was president of Pacific Gas and Electric). By no stretch of the imagination could he be thought of as a potential "Mr. Temple." Black later commented on their meeting, "I really wasn't very interested in meeting Shirley Temple. I was living a very full life of my own and—well, I just didn't care. I had never seen a Shirley Temple movie in my life."

As the wife of Charles Black, Shirley retired from the screen and took up a life which most people would describe as "society," a word she herself preferred not to use. "I don't think of the people around here as being "society" so much as people who *accomplish* something. We are mostly just young families. We just have a sense of community responsibility." (Real-estate agents in their wealthy San Francisco suburb, however, described the Blacks' set as "the young old fogies.")

John Agar had agreed not to see his daughter again, and she was later adopted by Black. In addition, the Blacks had two children of their own. Charles, Jr., was born April 28, 1952, at the Naval Hospital in Bethesda, Maryland, where Black was serving on active duty as a naval

With a Shirley Temple doll and daughter Lori in 1958

reserve officer during the Korean War. It was a difficult Caesarean section in which Shirley had been near death. On April 9, 1954, a daughter, Lori, was born in California.

For the next few years, Shirley Temple, the movie star, largely ceased to exist. In her place was a civic-minded, busy, and happy upper-class matron. If her eyes twinkled just a bit more than the average wife's and if her dimples looked remarkably familiar, still her identity was established, not as Shirley Temple, the eighth wonder of the world, but as

Mrs. Charles Black. As she had as a child, Shirley led a strict, simple life, well-ordered and obviously happy. She spent her time getting her family off to school in the morning, and then kept herself busy with various civic activities and charities, with time left over for golf, gardening, and interior decorating. The latter activity was a holdover from her movie days, and she said she had "learned the business from studying sets." She became a licensed professional, but commented ruefully, "I can't work for strangers. They just want to ask me about Elizabeth Taylor."

According to Hollywood legend, Darryl Zanuck once prophesied that Shirley Temple would "be good every year of her life as long as she lived." (A remark which might better be attributed to that famous mangler of the English language, Samuel "include-me-out" Goldwyn). Nobody really believed it, but when Shirley was coaxed out of retirement to launch her own television show, *Shirley Temple's Storybook*, on NBC in early 1958, it looked as if Zanuck might have been right. A ripe old twenty-nine, Shirley was a soft-looking matron, full-bosomed and darker-haired, but still warm and sparkly and able to warble a little tune. (The show's theme song, "Dreams Are Made for Children," was something she knew all about.) For the most part, Shirley merely introduced and narrated the lavishly mounted fairy tales the show presented, but she also acted in a few ("Legend of Sleepy Hollow" and "Mother Goose").

One of her most valuable assets was, of course, her publicity value. She gave out interview after interview, lacing each one with the candor that had delighted and intrigued newsmen when she was a child. Asked about her past career, Shirley remarked, "I have no sad memories. I never had to work very hard. We all just seemed to play games. But for the future," she shrewdly added, "it will be hard from now on—there will be competition." No statement could better sum up the difference between her childhood career and her adult attempt to equal it. To commemorate the return to show business by the biggest little girl of them all, Ideal Toys reissued that old favorite, the Shirley Temple Doll—this one a modern nylon-and-vinyl version.

The television series lasted a year, and Shirley received a salary plus a percentage of the profits. In 1960, she did *The Shirley Temple Show*, fourteen episodes which retold favorite children's stories. In the mid-sixties, she was announced for a television series called *Go Fight City Hall*, but it did not find a sponsor. This abortive pilot was her last work on television (except for guest appearances), but she enjoyed it. "I love the work, and Charles likes me to do it. I don't want to perpetuate a myth. I just enjoy it. I even like the air on the sound stages." Nevertheless, Shirley Temple was officially finished with show business, and as a kind of farewell statement, she told a reporter, "I am a family woman. I like to think back to the years when I was a child and remember that my parents never let my career interfere with the family relationship of my father, my mother, my brothers, and myself. And my most rewarding experiences today are the times I am with my husband and my children—and nobody else."

If it was good-bye to one kind of play-acting, it was "hello" to another. Shirley Black had always expressed definite opinions on the issues of the day. While serving on the board of the San Francisco Film Festival, she had resigned in protest over the type of films to be shown. (In particular, she was furious over the screening of Mai Zetterling's *Night Games,* which she considered pornographic.) She had been known to yank her children out of school programs and to leave movie theatres in a huff if she felt the film was unsuitable for her children. (Ironically, considering the run-down nannies and dead mothers of some of her own movies, she had once bawled a theatre manager out for showing a film in which the parents had been killed in an auto crash.)

In September of 1967, she found a new career . . . or tried to find a new career. Mrs. Black announced her candidacy for the Congressional seat vacated by the death of Representative J. Arthur Younger, State of California. She ran on the Republican ticket, and, in announcing her intentions, said at the outset, "Little Shirley Temple is not running. Make it Shirley Temple Black, Republican Independent."

Almost no one did, particularly newsmen who seized the opportunity to make jokes on her former film titles (Little Miss Candidate, Off to Congress on the Good Ship Lollipop, and Curly Top for Congress). Shirley Temple Black waged as dignified a campaign as she could, and her two main pronouncements concerned her feelings about Vietnam and Lyndon Johnson's "Great Society." On the former issue, her views were for the time rather direct and outside the main conservative stream: "It is not progress for the largest, strongest military power in the world to be mired down in apparently endless war with one of the smallest and weakest countries in the world." Although Mrs. Black naturally wanted the United States to "honor its commitments" in Asia, she stated strongly that it should be done quickly. She had more thoughts "on progress," particularly in those stormy days of the 1960's: "It is not progress when some of our citizens participate in bloody riots and burn down whole sections of cities; when pornography becomes big business and when our children are exposed to it."

Shirley outlined the other things she was against: high taxes, race riots, and drug-taking. She went on: "I'm neither a hawk nor a dove; I'm an owl. I feel if I am elected to Congress I cannot do much about this war, but I can do something to prevent the next Vietnam developing." Candidates running against Shirley naturally resented her easy entry to

With Charles Black at the United Nations

publicity during the campaign. One complained that he went all the way to a muddy Marine outpost near the DMZ to interview soldiers about the war. When he opened a copy of the latest GI newspaper, there was a photo of Shirley Temple Black, smugly pouring out coffee at a fund-raising gathering in Redwood City.

In campaigning for high office, Shirley showed more "show biz" flair than she ever had as an adult movie star. Despite her protests about not wanting to campaign as "little Shirley," she was shrewd enough to sneak in plenty of indirect references to her movie stardom, telling audiences that the Great Society was "a pretty bad movie" which had turned into a "flop." Shirley's campaign was helped out by two former co-stars, Governor Ronald Reagan and Senator George Murphy, and when Shirley expounded her theory that tuition should be paid by students at the University of California because, by working harder for their education, they would appreciate it more . . . somehow in the turbulent sixties, it all seemed like one of those "just around the corner" epics of the thirties. As the wealthy, slightly plump matron talked her way around the streets of San Francisco, evidently the voters thought so, too. Shirley Temple Black lost the election, and never did dance into that Big Candy Shop up on Capitol Hill.

Although she was defeated, Shirley had taken her loss with dignity and humor. Handicapped by amateur campaign management, late entry into the foray, poorly and hurriedly thought-out issues, and her own innocence in handling state-party factionalism—she had gone down to her first real defeat in life since her divorce from Agar.

Instead of giving up and returning to life as a suburban matron, Shirley Black decided to continue in the political field. In 1968, a Presidential election year, she volunteered for the Speakers Bureau of the National Republican Committee. She spoke sometimes as often as three times daily, traveling to twenty-one states, forty-six cities and even five foreign countries on behalf of her party. In 1969, her hard work and effectiveness were rewarded by the newly elected President Richard Nixon. She was given the prestigious designation of full deputy to the United Nations.

Shirley was not the first American delegate from the film colony— Irene Dunne had served before her—and traditionally, the U.S. delegation includes a well-known figure to bring publicity to the United Nations. But the question among other delegates was—would the former child-star just be a decoration . . . would she prove an embar-

On a trip to Amsterdam

rassment . . . or would she serve? No doubt to those who had known her throughout her life, it was a foolish question. Shirley Temple had never been anything in her life but a dutiful daughter, a willing learner, a devoted wife and mother, and—above all—a hard worker. She served.

After a few "getting acquainted" errors, such as speaking out without permission, having to improvise filibusters on topics she didn't know much about, and forgetting to vote as instructed, she soon proved herself an invaluable and well-informed negotiator. Within no time, or just about as much time as it used to take to straighten out the plots of her old movies, Shirley Black was dubbed "the United States' secret weapon." Ambassador Olds commented, "Her popularity and glamour as a former movie star helped. People were surprised at the toughness of her positions, but she prepared; that's what made her tough-minded." Her work on the Preparatory Committee for the United Nations Conference on the Human Environment, for which she served as Deputy Chairman, was particularly outstanding.

The Blacks had joined the Sierra Club in their San Francisco area in 1954. In the following years she began working closely with various conservation groups, including the National Wildlife Federation, and she was placed eventually on their Board of Directors. Her husband, who had successfully followed various business enterprises, became President of Mardela International, an aquaculture company involved in fisheries, and the research, development, and management of marine resources.

Mrs. Black also served on the International Federation of Multiple Sclerosis Societies, and found herself trapped in unfriendly territory in Prague during August of 1969, when the Russians took over the Prague airport. (She was there to negotiate Czechoslovakia's entry into the nineteen-nation federation.)

From September 1972 to January 1974, she served as special assistant to the chairman of the President's Council for Environmental Quality. Finally, as a culmination and final reward for her hard work and diplomacy, she was named to the prestigious post of United States Ambassador to Ghana, one of the last acts

On television with Mike Douglas, 1973

of the Nixon Administration in the summer of 1974.

In 1973, Shirley Temple Black made headlines when she courageously announced she had undergone major surgery for the removal of a breast which had developed a malignancy. Writing in a national women's magazine, she described her symptoms, the surgery she had undergone, as well as the emotional adjustment. She urged others: "Don't sit home and be afraid." By speaking out on an operation few women would wish to talk about in private, much less public print, she put aside both her privacy and her vanity in the hope of saving millions of women from unnecessary death. The resulting outpouring of love and respect which came to her following this statement was like a reminder of the old days—hundreds of telegrams, thousands of telephone messages, and more than 50,000 letters. She received praise and good wishes, support from fellow sufferers, many expressions of close identification, pleas for help from frightened women, and communications of all sorts from anti-cancer organizations.

With this new "career" as a crusader against cancer, she forged yet another avenue of public concern and interest for herself. In everything she had done as an adult, the ghost of little Shirley Temple had shadowed her accomplishments. This time, once and for all, the limelight belonged completely to the grown-up Shirley Temple Black. The letters and the love—as well as the respect—belonged to the woman, not the child.

I feel like I know her. I feel like she's a relative of mine. Yet I'm sort of detached and critical.

Mrs. Charles Black,
on viewing a
Shirley Temple movie.

CURTAIN CALL: LADY, TAKE A BOW!

"I'm a pushover for fairy tales," Shirley Temple Black once remarked, and it's no wonder. Hollywood legend says that early fame and later happiness are mutually exclusive, but Shirley Temple defied that myth just as she once defied the odds against becoming a star. Her life is the American dream of success rewritten with an uncharacteristic happy ending.

"People can be ruined by becoming too successful at the wrong age," Mrs. Black admits, but she has her own reasons why she escaped. "I started working at age three, and at that age it seemed very natural —like 'Doesn't everybody make movies?' I didn't know the difference . . . I had the best kind of childhood anyone could have. Instead of having all the great stories of myth and fiction read to me, it was possible for me to actually live the parts. . . . When I was young, Mother never showed me any stories about myself in magazines or newspapers. Later I could read them if I wished. After reading a few I stopped. I was recognizable in them, but somehow it was always some other person's concept of Shir-

ley Temple, and in many cases, an idealization. . . . I'm no princess, or tin goddess, and I wouldn't want to be one either. I've had a good life and a fortunate one. I like to feel that I've brought people pleasure on the screen. But it was an accident of fate, of timing, that gave me my chance."

Today, Shirley Temple Black takes a matter-of-fact attitude toward her former fame. ("I try to enjoy it for whatever I can.") She is not the "myth-on-the-hoof" that some ex-film stars are—she is, after all, no longer a child. But the legend of little Shirley Temple lives on, an image which someone once said equaled the Statue of Liberty in gross tonnage (although in terms of her political career, a more apt comparison might be the *Titanic*). Shirley Temple Black faces those "Didn't you used to be Shirley Temple?" inquiries with equanimity. She remains cheerful when men old enough to be her father tell her they loved her on the screen "when they were little boys." She listens patiently when people claim they once bounced her on their knees . . . or "met her in a bar" when she was not old enough for the Junior League, much less the cocktail lounge. She graciously thanks the

142

couple that sends over to her table the millionth "Shirley Temple" as a "cute idea" and smilingly refuses her ten-millionth request to sing "On the Good Ship Lollipop" just once—for old time's sake. ("You know, I got awfully tired of singing that—even as a kid.") Perhaps her memories of the old days are best represented by the revealing remarks made when she visited the southern manor house set that was used in *The Littlest Rebel*: "I used to think of the mansion as an overwhelming edifice with towering white columns. But a few years ago I visited it and the building had shrunk, the columns were skinny, and the porch was narrow." As to her old movies, she makes a flat statement, "We don't run them at home anymore."

In some ways, Shirley Temple seems to have grown up to be her own mother. Like Gertrude Temple before her, she is now an attractive woman who fiercely protects her family from exploitation. "I have a mean eye. Mixed-up people still come around. A man came to the door the other day and said he'd married me in 1940 and sold his stamp collection to get here." Gertrude Temple adds, "I always have to ask her permission to talk to interviewers, and she sizes everybody up very thoroughly."

In answer to those inevitable questions, yes, indeed, she *used* to be Shirley Temple, but in her own mind the little tot belongs to the past. And *that's* whatever happened to the world's most famous child star. She grew up. And when she grew up, she became Shirley Temple Black. In her quiet way, she is making that name nearly as famous as the other one. Besides being an ambassador, a UN delegate, an ardent conservationist, and a cancer crusader, she is a vivacious woman who looks young for her years and who speaks with spirit and more wit than anyone seems willing to give a former child star credit for. She is a happy and satisfied woman, still the odds breaker. In this day and age—particularly considering her Hollywood background—that seems to qualify her as, if no longer little Miss Miracle, then certainly at least Ms. Surprise Ending. Or as the merrily singing voices trill at the end of *The Littlest Rebel*, "Everything went wrong . . . but it turned out right . . . sing polly wolly doodle all the day!"

> *I won't go backwards . . .*
> *I'm going ahead.*
> Shirley Temple Black

144

BIBLIOGRAPHY

Alexander, Shana. "Little Shirley Temple Lives," *Life*, November 3, 1967.

Arnold, Maxine. "Super Matron," *Photoplay*, April 1946, p. 39.

Baskette, Kirtley. "The Amazing Temple Family," *Photoplay*, April 1936, Vol. XLIX, No. 4, p. 14.

Behlmer, Rudy. *Memo from David O. Selznick*, Viking, New York, 1972.

Black, Shirley Temple. "When I Was 17," *Seventeen*, October 1971.

——————. "Prague Diary," *McCalls*, January 1969.

Bogdanovich, Peter. *Allan Dwan, the last pioneer*, Praeger Film Library, New York, 1971.

——————. *John Ford*, Movie Paperbacks, University of California Press, 1968.

Burdick, Loraine. *Shirley's Toys*, Quest-Eridon Books, Washington, 1973.

——————. *Shirley's Dolls*, Quest-Eridon Books, Washington, 1973.

Caplan, G. "Outpouring of Love for Shirley Temple Black," *McCalls*, March 1973.

Downing, "Talk About Agar," *Photoplay*, November 1948, p. 44.

Foster, C.J., "Mrs. Temple on Bringing Up Shirley," *Parents*, October 1938.

Ghidalia, Mickey. "Good Luck, Shirley!," *Modern Screen*, July 1945, p. 34.

Goodman, Ezra. *The Fifty-Year Decline and Fall of Hollywood*, MacFadden, New York, 1962.

Greene, Graham. *Graham Greene on Film*, Collected Film Criticism, 1935-1939, Simon and Schuster, New York, 1972.

Hess, J. "Shirley Temple Black: Gentle Crusader," *National Wildlife*, December 1973.

Jackson, Michael. "Protecting the Future of the Greatest Little Star," *Photoplay*, March 1937, Vol. LI, No. 3, p. 26.

Janis, Elsie. "Shirley in Short," *Photoplay*, March 1945, p. 38.

——————. "Junior Mrs.", *Modern Screen*, December 1945, p. 40.

Karr, Jeanne. "Senior Miss," *Modern Screen*, October 1943, p. 46.

Kevles, Barbara. "Shirley Temple Black in 'A U.S. Diplomat at the U.N.,' " *Saturday Evening Post*, Summer 1972.

Lowrance, Dee. "Great Expectations," *Modern Screen*, December 1947.

Maltin, Leonard. "Jack Haley Today," *Film Fan Monthly*, September 1971.

——————. *The Great Movie Shorts*, Crown, New York, 1972.

Markel, Helen. "Goldilocks Grows Up . . . But Definitely," *New York Times Magazine*, February 11, 1945.

Maxwell, Elsa. "This You Must Understand," *Photoplay*, February 1950, p. 34.

Miller, Cynthia. "Life with Mother," *Modern Screen*, March 1945, p. 34.

Ormiston, Roberta. "Hawaiian Love Song," *Photoplay*, February 1951, p. 33.

Parish, James Robert. *The Fox Girls*, Arlington House, New York, 1971.

Parsons, Louella. "At the Turn of the Teens," *Photoplay*, June 1944, p. 33.

——————. "Shirley's Baby," *Photoplay*, April 1948, p. 33.

——————. "The John Agar Puzzle," *Photoplay*, May 1951, p. 44.

——————. "What Happened to the Temple Marriage," *Photoplay*, December 1949, p. 32.

——————. "Peewee's Progress," cover story, *Time*, April 27, 1936.

Pieck, Kaaren. "Since They Went Away," *Modern Screen*, April 1944, p. 48.

Ringgold, Gene. "Shirley Temple," *Screen Facts*, Vol. 2, No. 6, 1965.

Schickel, Richard. "Shirley or Curley?," *Life*, January 13, 1969.

Service, Faith. "First Kiss—and Miss Temple," *Photoplay*, June 1942, p. 41.

Shipman, David. *The Great Movie Stars, The Golden Years*, Bonanza, New York, 1972.

Shipp, Cameron. "Big Girl," *Photoplay*, September 1946, p. 56.

——————. "Sixteen's Okay," *Modern Screen*, November 1944, p. 42.

Smalley, Jack. "Myth Shirley Temple," *Photoplay*, September 1937, Vol. LI, No. 9, p. 36.

Temple, Shirley. "A Letter to My Daughter," *Photoplay*, May 1949, p. 68.

——————. "Don't Sit Home & Be Afraid," *McCalls*, February 1973.

——————. "For My Baby," *Photoplay*, March 1948, p. 44.

——————. "The Shirley I Know," *Photoplay*, November 1937, p. 64.

Waterbury, Ruth. "Shirley, Lohengrin and Happiness," *Photoplay*, December 1945, p. 28.

——————. "The Love Story of Shirley and Her Sergeant," *Photoplay*, July 1945, p. 56.

Zeitlin, Ida. "Living Is Fun!" *Photoplay*, November 1950, p. 38.

Zierold, Norman J., *The Child Stars*, Coward-McCann, New York, 1965.

THE FILMS OF SHIRLEY TEMPLE

The director's name follows the release date. A (c) following the release date indicates that the film was in color. Sp indicates screenplay and b/o indicates based/on.

THE SHORT FILMS

Educational Films. Producer and Supervisor: Jack Hays. Director: Charles Lamont.

"The Baby Burlesks"	WAR BABIES. 1932.
	THE RUNT PAGE. 1932.
	PIE COVERED WAGON. 1932.
	GLAD RAGS TO RICHES. 1932.
	KID'S LAST FIGHT. 1933.
	KID'IN' HOLLYWOOD. 1933
	POLLY-TIX IN WASHINGTON. 1933.
	KID' IN' AFRICA. 1933.
"Frolics of Youth"	MERRILY YOURS. 1933.
	PARDON MY PUPS. 1934
	MANAGED MONEY. 1934.
"Andy Clyde Series"	DORA'S DUNKIN' DONUTS. 1933.

Paramount. NEW DEAL RHYTHM. (Musical Featurette). 1934.
Astor Films. OUR GIRL SHIRLEY. (Compilation, 33 minutes of the Educational Films shorts). 1935.

THE FEATURE FILMS

15. RED-HAIRED ALIBI, Tower Production (released by Capital Films Exchange), 1932. *Christy Cabanne,* b/o novel by Wilson Collison. Cast: Merna Kennedy, Theodor von Eltz, Grant Withers, Purnell Pratt, Huntley Gordon, Fred Kelsey, John Vosburgh.

16. TO THE LAST MAN, Paramount, 1933. *Henry Hathaway.* Sp: Jack Cunningham, b/o novel by Zane Grey. Cast: Randolph Scott, Jack LaRue, Esther Ralston, Buster Crabbe, Noah Beery, Barton MacLane, Muriel Kirkland, Fuzzy Knight, Gail Patrick, Egon Brecher. Also filmed in 1923.

17. OUT ALL NIGHT, Universal, 1933. *Sam Taylor.* Sp: William Anthony McGuire, b/o story by Tim Whalen. Cast: Slim Summerville, ZaSu Pitts, Laura Hope Crews, Shirley Grey, Alexander Carr, Rollo Lloyd, Gene Lewis, Billy Barty.

18.   CAROLINA, Fox, 1934. *Henry King*. Sp: Reginald Berkeley, b/o play *The House of Connelly* by Paul Green. Cast: Janet Gaynor, Lionel Barrymore, Robert Young, Richard Cromwell, Henrietta Crosman, Mona Barrie, Stepin Fetchit, Russell Simpson.

19.   MANDALAY, Warner Brothers-First National, 1934. *Michael Curtiz*. Sp: Austin Parker and Charles Kenyon, b/o story by Paul Hervey Fox. Cast: Kay Francis, Ricardo Cortez, Warner Oland, Lyle Talbot, Ruth Donnelly, Reginald Owen, Hobart Cavanaugh, David Torrence, Rafaela Ottiano, Halliwell Hobbes, Etienne Girardot.

20.   STAND UP AND CHEER *(Fox Movietone Follies)*, Fox, 1934. *Hamilton MacFadden*. Sp: Ralph Spence, b/o story outline by Will Rogers and Philip Klein. Cast: Warner Baxter, Madge Evans, James Dunn, Sylvia Froos, John Boles, Arthur Byron, Ralph Morgan, Aunt Jemima, Nick Foran, Nigel Bruce, Stepin Fetchit.

21.   NOW I'LL TELL, Fox, 1934. *Edwin Burke*. Sp: Edwin Burke, b/o book by Mrs. Arnold Rothstein. Cast: Spencer Tracy, Helen Twelvetrees, Alice Faye, Robert Gleckler, Hobart Cavanaugh, Henry O'Neill, G.P. Huntley, Jr., Ronnie Cosbey, Ray Cooke, Frank Marlowe, Clarence Wilson.

22.   CHANGE OF HEART, Fox, 1934. *John G. Blystone*. Sp: Sonya Levien and James Gleason, b/o novel *Manhattan Love Song* by Kathleen Norris. Cast: Janet Gaynor, Charles Farrell, James Dunn, Ginger Rogers, Beryl Mercer, Gustav von Seyffertitz, Irene Franklin, Kenneth Thomson, Theodor von Eltz, Jane Darwell, Nella Walker.

23.   LITTLE MISS MARKER, Paramount, 1934. *Alexander Hall*. Sp: William R. Lipman, Sam Hellman, Gladys Lehman, b/o story by Damon Runyon. Cast: Adolphe Menjou, Dorothy Dell, Charles Bickford, Lynne Overman, Frank McGlynn, Sr., Tammany Young, Sam Hardy, Jack Sheehan. Remade in 1949 as *Sorrowful Jones*, and in 1963 as *40 Pounds of Trouble*.

24.   BABY, TAKE A BOW, Fox, 1934. *Harry Lachman*. Sp: Philip Klein and E.E. Paramore, Jr., b/o play *Square Crooks* by James P. Judge. Cast: James Dunn, Claire Trevor, Alan Dinehart, Ray Walker, Dorothy Libaire, Ralf Harolde, James Flavin.

25.   NOW AND FOREVER, Paramount, 1934. *Henry Hathaway*. Sp: Vincent Lawrence and Sylvia Thalberg, b/o story by Jack Kirkland and Melville Baker. Cast: Gary Cooper, Carole Lombard, Sir Guy Standing, Charlotte Granville, Gilbert Emery, Henry Kolker.

26.   BRIGHT EYES, Fox, 1934. *David Butler*. Sp: William Conselman, b/o story by David Butler, Edwin Burke. Cast: James Dunn, Judith Allen, Lois Wilson, Jane Withers, Theodor von Eltz, Charles Sellon, Jane Darwell.

27. THE LITTLE COLONEL, Fox, 1935. *David Butler*. Sp and adaptation: William Conselman, b/o story "The Little Colonel" by Annie Fellows Johnston. Cast: Lionel Barrymore, Evelyn Venable, John Lodge, Bill Robinson, Hattie McDaniel, William Burress, Sidney Blackmer. Color sequence by Technicolor.

28. OUR LITTLE GIRL, Fox, 1935. *John Robertson*. Sp: Stephen Avery, Allen Rivkin, b/o story "Heaven's Gate" by Florence Leighton Pfalzgraf. Cast: Rosemary Ames, Joel McCrea, Lyle Talbot, Erin O'Brien-Moore, J. Farrell MacDonald, Rita Owin.

29. CURLY TOP, Fox, 1935. *Irving Cummings*. Sp: Patterson McNutt and Arthur Beckhard. Cast: John Boles, Rochelle Hudson, Jane Darwell, Rafaela Ottiano, Esther Dale, Arthur Treacher, Etienne Girardot, Maurice Murphy.

30. THE LITTLEST REBEL, 20th Century-Fox, 1935. *David Butler*. Sp: Edwin Burke, b/o play by Edward Peple. Cast: John Boles, Jack Holt, Karen Morley, Bill Robinson, Guinn Williams, Willie Best, Frank McGlynn, Sr.

31. CAPTAIN JANUARY, 20th Century-Fox, 1936. *David Butler*. Sp: Sam Hellman, Gladys Lehman, Harry Tugend, b/o story by Laura E. Richards. Cast: Guy Kibbee, Slim Summerville, Buddy Ebsen, June Lang, Sara Haden, Jane Darwell. Also filmed in 1924.

32. POOR LITTLE RICH GIRL, 20th Century-Fox, 1936. *Irving Cummings*. Sp: Sam Hellman, Gladys Lehman, Harry Tugend, b/o stories by Eleanor Gates. Cast: Alice Faye, Gloria Stuart, Jack Haley, Michael Whalen, Sara Haden, Jane Darwell, Claude Gillingwater, Paul Stanton, Henry Armetta. Also filmed in 1917.

33. DIMPLES, 20th Century-Fox, 1936. *William A. Seiter*. Sp: Arthur Sheekman and Nat Perrin. Cast: Frank Morgan, Helen Westley, Berton Churchill, Robert Kent, Delma Byron, Astrid Allwyn, Julius Tannen.

34. STOWAWAY, 20th Century-Fox, 1936. *William A. Seiter*. Sp: William Conselman, Arthur Sheekman, and Nat Perrin, b/o story by Samuel G. Engel. Cast: Robert Young, Alice Faye, Eugene Pallette, Helen Westley, Arthur Treacher, J. Edward Bromberg, Astrid Allwyn, Allan Lane, Robert Greig.

35. WEE WILLIE WINKIE, 20th Century-Fox, 1937. *John Ford*. Sp: Ernest Pascal and Julien Josephson, b/o story by Rudyard Kipling. Cast: Victor McLaglen, C. Aubrey Smith, June Lang, Michael Whalen, Cesar Romero, Constance Collier, Douglas Scott, Gavin Muir.

36.   HEIDI, 20th Century-Fox, 1937. *Allan Dwan*. Sp: Walter Ferris and Julien Josephson, b/o novel by Johanna Spyri. Cast: Jean Hersholt, Arthur Treacher, Helen Westley, Pauline Moore. Thomas Beck, Mary Nash, Mady Christians, Sig Rumann, Marcia Mae Jones. Also filmed in 1953 and 1968.

37.   REBECCA OF SUNNYBROOK FARM, 20th Century-Fox, 1938. *Allan Dwan*. Sp: Karl Tunberg and Don Ettlinger, suggested by the Kate Douglas Wiggin story. Cast: Randolph Scott, Jack Haley, Gloria Stuart, Phyllis Brooks, Helen Westley, Slim Summerville, Bill Robinson, J. Edward Bromberg, Alan Dinehart, Dixie Dunbar, William Demarest. Also filmed in 1917 and 1932.

38.   LITTLE MISS BROADWAY, 20th Century-Fox, 1938. *Irving Cummings*. Sp: Harry Tugend and Jack Yellen. Cast: George Murphy, Jimmy Durante, Phyllis Brooks, Edna May Oliver, George Barbier, Edward Ellis, Jane Darwell, El Brendel, Donald Meek, Claude Gillingwater.

39.   JUST AROUND THE CORNER, 20th Century-Fox, 1938. *Irving Cummings*. Sp: Ethel Hill, J.P. McEvoy, and Darrell Ware, b/o story by Paul Gerard Smith. Cast: Charles Farrell, Joan Davis, Amanda Duff, Bill Robinson, Bert Lahr, Franklin Pangborn, Cora Witherspoon, Claude Gillingwater.

40.   THE LITTLE PRINCESS, 20th Century-Fox, 1939 (c). *Walter Lang*. Sp: Ethel Hill and Walter Ferris, b/o novel by Frances Hodgson Burnett. Cast: Richard Greene, Anita Louise, Ian Hunter, Cesar Romero, Arthur Treacher, Mary Nash, Sybil Jason, Miles Mander, Marcia Mae Jones, Beryl Mercer, E.E. Clive. Also filmed in 1917.

41.   SUSANNAH OF THE MOUNTIES, 20th Century-Fox, 1938 (sepiatone). *William A. Seiter*. Sp: Robert Ellis and Helen Logan, b/o story by Fidel La Barba and Walter Ferris and book by Muriel Denison. Cast: Randolph Scott, Margaret Lockwood, Martin Good Rider, J. Farrell MacDonald, Maurice Moscovich, Moroni Olsen, Victor Jory.

42.   THE BLUE BIRD, 20th Century-Fox, 1940 (c). *Walter Lang*. Sp: Ernest Pascal, b/o play by Maurice Maeterlinck. Cast: Spring Byington, Nigel Bruce, Gale Sondergaard, Eddie Collins, Sybil Jason, Jessie Ralph, Helen Ericson, Johnny Russell, Laura Hope Crews.

43.   YOUNG PEOPLE, 20th Century-Fox, 1940. *Allan Dwan*. Sp: Edwin Blum and Don Ettlinger. Cast: Jack Oakie, Charlotte Greenwood, Arleen Whelan, George Montgomery, Kathleen Howard, Minor Watson, Frank Swann, Frank Sully, Mae Marsh.

44. KATHLEEN, Metro-Goldwyn-Mayer, 1941. *Harold S. Bucquet*. Sp: Mary McCall, Jr., b/o story by Kay Van Riper. Cast: Laraine Day, Herbert Marshall, Gail Patrick, Felix Bressart, Nella Walker, Lloyd Corrigan.

45. MISS ANNIE ROONEY, An Edward Small Production, released by United Artists, 1942. *Edwin L. Marin*. Sp: George Bruce. Cast: William Gargan, Guy Kibbee, Dickie Moore, Peggy Ryan, Roland DuPree, Gloria Holden, Jonathan Hale, Mary Field, June Lockhart.

46. SINCE YOU WENT AWAY, A David O. Selznick Production, released by United Artists, 1944. *John Cromwell*. Sp: David O. Selznick, b/o novel by Margaret Buell Wilder. Cast: Claudette Colbert, Jennifer Jones, Joseph Cotten, Monty Woolley, Lionel Barrymore, Robert Walker, Agnes Moorehead, Hattie McDaniel, Guy Madison, Craig Stevens, Keenan Wynn, Albert Basserman, Nazimova.

47. I'LL BE SEEING YOU, A David O. Selznick Production, released by United Artists, 1944. *William Dieterle*. Sp: Marion Parsonnet, b/o radio play by Charles Martin. Cast: Ginger Rogers, Joseph Cotten, Spring Byington, Tom Tully, Chill Wills, Dare Harris, Kenny Bowers.

48. KISS AND TELL, Columbia, 1945. *Richard Wallace*. Sp: F. Hugh Herbert, b/o his play. Cast: Jerome Courtland, Walter Abel, Katharine Alexander, Robert Benchley, Porter Hall, Tom Tully, Darryl Hickman, Scott Elliott, Virginia Welles.

49. HONEYMOON, RKO, 1947. *William Keighley*. Sp: Michael Kanin, b/o story by Vicki Baum. Cast: Franchot Tone, Guy Madison, Lina Romay, Gene Lockhart, Corinna Mura, Grant Mitchell.

50. THE BACHELOR AND THE BOBBY-SOXER, RKO, 1947. *Irving Reis*. Sp and story: Sidney Sheldon. Cast: Myrna Loy, Cary Grant, Rudy Vallee, Ray Collins, Harry Davenport, Johnny Sands, Don Beddoe, Lillian Randolph, Veda Ann Borg, Dan Tobin.

51. THAT HAGEN GIRL, Warner Brothers, 1947. *Peter Godfrey*. Sp: Charles Hoffman, b/o novel by Edith Roberts. Cast: Ronald Reagan, Rory Calhoun, Lois Maxwell, Dorothy Peterson, Charles Kemper, Conrad Janis, Penny Edwards, Jean Porter, Harry Davenport.

52. FORT APACHE, RKO, 1948. *John Ford*. Sp: Frank S. Nugent, b/o novel *Massacre* by James Warner Bellah. Cast: Henry Fonda, John Wayne, John Agar, Pedro Armendariz, Ward Bond, Irene Rich, George O'Brien, Anna Lee, Victor McLaglen, Dick Foran, Jack Pennick, Guy Kibbee.

53.   MR. BELVEDERE GOES TO COLLEGE, 20th Century-Fox, 1949. *Elliott Nugent*. Sp: Richard Sale, Mary Loos, and Mary McCall, Jr., b/o characters created by Gwen Davenport. Cast: Clifton Webb, Tom Drake, Alan Young, Jessie Royce Landis, Kathleen Hughes, Taylor Holmes, Jeff Chandler, Sally Forrest.

54.   ADVENTURE IN BALTIMORE, RKO, 1949. *Richard Wallace*. Sp: Lionel Houser, b/o story by Christopher Isherwood and Lesser Samuels. Cast: Robert Young, John Agar, Albert Sharpe, Josephine Hutchinson, Charles Kemper, Johnny Sands, John Miljan, Norma Varden.

55.   THE STORY OF SEABISCUIT, Warner Brothers, 1949. *David Butler*. Sp: John Taintor Foote, b/o his story. Cast: Barry Fitzgerald, Lon McCallister, Rosemary DeCamp, Donald McBride, Pierre Watkin, William Forrest.

56.   A KISS FOR CORLISS, A Strand Production, released by United Artists, 1949. *Richard Wallace*. Sp: Howard Dimsdale, b/o characters created by F. Hugh Herbert. Cast: David Niven, Tom Tully, Virginia Welles, Darryl Hickman, Robert Ellis, Richard Gaines, Gloria Holden, Kathryn Card, Roy Roberts.

In addition, a clip of Shirley Temple's number from *Stand Up and Cheer* ("Baby, Take a Bow") was used in the 1944 20th Century-Fox Production, *Take It or Leave It*, based on Phil Baker's popular radio show. Directed by Benjamin Stoloff, starring Phil Baker, Edward Ryan, Marjorie Massow.

Shirley Temple also appeared as herself in the 1938 motion picture self-promotional short, *The World is Ours*.

INDEX

156

157

Pyramid's Illustrated History of the Movies

a beautiful, original series of enchanting volumes on your favorite stars and motion pictures. Each book is superbly written and contains dozens of exciting photos! They are available from your local dealer, or you can use this page to order direct.

_____**CHARLIE CHAPLIN** • Robert F. Moss • M3640 • $1.75 • The irrepressible Tramp known everywhere as a vastly comic and eloquent star.

_____**BARBARA STANWYCK** • Jerry Vermilye • M3641 • $1.75 • Tough or sentimental, vicious or vulnerable, she was always the great actress.

_____**EDWARD G. ROBINSON** • Foster Hirsch • M3642 • $1.75 • Unsurpassed for his vigorous, powerful performances in nearly ninety films.

_____**SHIRLEY TEMPLE** • Jeanine Basinger • M3643 • $1.75 • The child star who sang, danced, smiled and pouted her way into the hearts of millions.

_____**GRETA GARBO** • Richard Corliss • M3480 • $1.75 • The star who set the screen aglow with her beauty and artistry.

_____**JOHN WAYNE** • Alan G. Barbour • M3481 • $1.75 • For nearly fifty years, the film's ideal of courage and "true grit".

_____**CARY GRANT** • Jerry Vermilye • M3246 • $1.75 • An overview of this most popular star from the early years up through the 60's.

_____**ELIZABETH TAYLOR** • Foster Hirsch • M3247 • $1.75 • The screen's most beautiful woman. Her films from a young girl to a foul-mouthed harridan.

_____**SPENCER TRACY** • Romano Tozzi • M3248 • $1.75 • Sincere and honest, in private and before the public.

_____**GANGSTERS** • John Gabree • M3249 • $1.75 • Raw violence and excitement over the last 40 years.

_____**KARLOFF AND COMPANY: THE HORROR FILM** • Robert Moss • M3415 • $1.75 • Astute appraisal of the ghouls, ghosts and maniacs of the horror film.

_____**BETTE DAVIS** • Jerry Vermilye • M2932 • $1.75 Vivid, flamboyant and thoroughly professional. An appraisal of her 80 films.

_____**CLARK GABLE** • René Jordan • M2929 • $1.75 • Examination of his more than sixty films in which he reigned as "King of the Movies."

_____**KATHARINE HEPBURN** • Alvin H. Marill • M2931 • $1.75 • A pentrating look at the enchanting comedienne and the brilliant dramatic actress.

_____**HUMPHREY BOGART** • Alan G. Barbour • M2930 • $1.75 • A look at the man, the actor and the myth.

_____**JUDY GARLAND** • James Juneau • M3482 • $1.75 • The electrifying singer who traveled "over the rainbow".

_____**THE WAR FILM** • Norman Kagan • M3483 • $1.75 • The memorable films conveying all the brutality, courage and folly of war.

_____**MARLENE DIETRICH** • Charles Silver • M3484 • $1.75 • The alluring enchantress with her unique aura of mystery and glamour.

_____**JAMES STEWART** • Howard Thompson • M3485 • $1.75 • The ideal of warmth and sincerity during more than forty years of films.

_____**W. C. FIELDS** • Nicholas Yanni • M3486 • $1.75 • The comic genius with the larger-than-life style and personality.

_____**THE MOVIE MUSICAL** • Lee Edward Stern • M3487 • $1.75 • From the dazzle and glitter of the thirties to today's widescreen opulence.

_____**GARY COOPER** • René Jordan • M3416 • $1.75 • Moving portrait of America's most stalwart screen hero.

_____**JOAN CRAWFORD** • Stephen Harvey • M3417 • $1.75 • Indomitable and vulnerable, Crawford has enchanted filmgoers for over four decades.

_____**MARLON BRANDO** • René Jordan • M3128 • $1.75 • A look at the definitive screen "rebel", from the fifties to LAST TANGO.

_____**MARILYN MONROE** • Joan Mellen • M3129 • $1.75 • Compassionate look at this deeply sensitive and very vulnerable woman.

_____**INGRID BERGMAN** • Curtis F. Brown • M3130 • $1.75 • Extraordinary and stormy — a look at Bergman's more than forty films.

_____**JAMES CAGNEY** • Andrew Bergman • M3127 • $1.75 • Ruthless gangster to nimble song-and-dance man.

_____**PAUL NEWMAN** • Michael Kerbel • M3418 • $1.75 • The rebel, the renegade and the ruthless opportunist — a very sensitive analysis of a very popular actor.

Indicate the number of each title desired and **send this page** with check or money order to:
PYRAMID BOOKS, Dept. MB. 9 Garden St. Moonachie, N.J. 07074

I enclose a check or money order for $_____, which includes the **total price** of the books ordered plus **50¢ additional per book** for postage and handling **if I have ordered less than 4 books**. If I have ordered 4 books or more, I understand that the publisher will pay all postage and handling.

MY NAME_____

ADDRESS_____

CITY_____

STATE_____ ZIP_____

ABOUT THE AUTHOR
Jeanine Basinger is a Lecturer in American Film History at Wesleyan University in Middletown, Connecticut, where she has taught courses on the studio system, the auteur theory, film genres, and directional style. Her writings have appeared in many publications, including *The New York Times*, *Film Fan Monthly*, and the American Film Institute *Report*.

ABOUT THE EDITOR
Ted Sennett is the author of *Warner Brothers Presents*, a tribute to the great Warners films of the Thirties and Forties, and of *Lunatics and Lovers*, on the long-vanished but well-remembered "screwball" comedies of the past. He is also the editor of *The Movie Buff's Book* and has written about films for magazines and newspapers. He lives in New Jersey with his wife and three children.